Orthodox Perspectives on Mission

TO HIS ALL-HOLINESS BARTHOLOMEW I
A LONG-TIME FRIEND AND COMPANION IN ECUMENICAL STRUGGLE
ON THE OCCASION OF HIS ELECTION AS ECUMENICAL PATRIARCH

Orthodox Perspectives on Mission

Archbishop Aram Keshishian

REGNUM
LYNX

Published by
Regnum Books
PO Box 70, Oxford, OX2 6HB

in association with
Lynx Communications
Sandy Lane West, Oxford, England
ISBN 0 7459 2685 1

First edition 1992

A catalogue record for this book is available
from the British Library

Printed and bound in Great Britain

Contents

Foreword

Clarity of thought, a unique spiritual leadership deeply rooted in a commitment to Jesus Christ and his church, as well as a keen awareness of how the apostolic faith revealed and confessed needs to be lived out in the day-to-day witness of the church in unity and mission: these are the marks of His Eminence Archbishop Aram Keshishian, the Primate of the Armenian Orthodox Church in Lebanon and the current Moderator of the Central Committee of the World Council of Churches. H.E. Archbishop Aram Keshishian has been appointed to the office of the Moderator for such a time as this, and the thoughts expressed in the articles and papers published in this book give ample evidence of his courage and humility. He articulates his thoughts and concerns with clarity and boldness and the global Christian family does well to read and heed what is expressed. The views, perspectives and challenges, systematically and vividly displayed in this volume, clearly document the author as an outstanding Oriental Orthodox theologian and ecumenical statesman, who, deeply rooted in his centuries-old tradition, knows how to make the Christian faith and gospel relevant in our modern, and increasingly complex, societies.

Orthodox Perspectives on Mission is a collection of various articles and papers given at Orthodox and ecumenical conferences and consultations during the last decade or so. They give a rare insight into the vital theological and ecclesiological concerns and perspectives of the Orthodox family of churches on many ecumenical issues and questions which tend to be on today's ecumenical agenda. H.E. Aram Keshishian raises the question of what God's agenda for all of us should be, and how we need to seek God's will and answers for our time and age.

The Armenian Apostolic Church, whose Primate of Lebanon H.E. Archbishop Aram Keshishian is, has faithfully kept the apostolic tradition in the midst of much persecution throughout its history. A major concern of Orthodox theology has been to faithfully interpret Christian love and faith in the Trinitarian tradition of the undivided church. For the Orthodox Church, as well as for evangelical Christians around the globe, the gospel of Jesus Christ—his incarnation, crucifixion and resurrection—is normative for salvation and God's saving acts in history. *Orthodox Perspectives on Mission* illustrates how important the Orthodox contribution is to the wider ecumenical family, counteracting much prevailing excessive Christocentricism, theological rationalism and liberalism, as well as ecclesiological institutionalism which often lacks an understanding of the call for unity in the one, holy, universal and apostolic church. It is well to remind ourselves that it is the Orthodox Church which confronted the entrenched paganism of the Roman and Hellenistic cultures. The spirituality and theological depth expressed in the articles of this book well document that the spiritual and intellectual resources of the Orthodox family of churches have once more a vital role to play towards a true missionary encounter with the prevailing culture of modernity which is in such great need of the gospel.

This book deserves therefore a wide distribution and careful reading by Christians from various traditions, inside and outside the fellowship of the World Council of Churches. The Orthodox perception concerning the perplexities and challenges of our day and age, as well as the insightful interaction with the problems and issues confronting the ecumenical family, needs to be considered carefully by all Christians who are concerned for an authentic witness in mission and unity. Our mutual interrelatedness in the one body of Christ calls us to widen our horizons and our awareness of one another. It is through the work of the Holy Spirit, in answer to the prayer of Christ, who yearns to see us grow in unity and love, that new channels of communication and understanding are opening for the universal church to meet across many painful divisions. The World Council of Churches has been a unique instrument of such fellowship, bringing divided churches together so that they may mutually recognize elements of the true church and thus provoke one another towards visible unity.

The converging thoughts and theological concerns expressed both in an Orthodox statement on *Reflections of Orthodox Participants* and an open letter on *Evangelical Perspectives from Canberra*, during the seventh assembly of the World Council of Churches in Canberra, Australia, in February 1991, referred to in this book, clearly exemplify how important it is for evangelical and all Protestant Christians to meet and understand the Orthodox Churches. It is therefore my hope and prayer that many Christians in the ecumenical and evangelical movements may through the careful reading of this book grow in a new understanding and appreciation of the Orthodox family of churches and their vital contribution to Christian thought, life and action.

I therefore highly recommend these deliberations by H.E. Aram Keshishian. The edification and challenges expressed in *Orthodox Perspectives on Mission* bear witness to genuine concern for spiritual renewal and a fresh desire for the glory of God to be manifested in the universal church in such a way that we all may grow in the grace of our Lord Jesus Christ, and the love of God, and the fellowship of the Holy Spirit.

The Revd Walter Arnold
Stuttgart, August 1992
Executive Secretary for Missions and Ecumenical Relations
Evangelical-Lutheran Church of Württemberg

Preface

This book is neither an exposition of formal Orthodox views and positions nor a substantial Orthodox contribution to the ecumenical discussion. It is simply an attempt of limited scope to look from an Orthodox perspective at some of the ecumenical themes and concerns which have acquired predominance, particularly during the last decade, in the life, thought and work of the World Council of Churches, and in the ecumenical movement at large. The papers included in this volume can be divided into six main groups:

1. The first three papers, namely *Justice, Peace and Creation, a Biblical Approach, Justice, Peace and Integrity of Creation in a Eucharistic Perspective* and *Human beings in Creation* deal, from different angles, with an important ecumenical process of reflection and action that came to be known as 'Justice, peace and the integrity of creation' (JPIC). Launched by the sixth assembly of the World Council of Churches (Vancouver, 1983), this process with its theological, ecological and socio-political dimensions and implications became, and continues to be, a major ecumenical priority both within and outside the constituency of the WCC.

2. The second group which includes '*Come, Holy Spirit, Renew the Whole Creation*', and *The Holy Spirit in Orthodox Pneumatology*, is a contribution to the theme of the seventh assembly of the WCC (Canberra, 1991) made in the context of the assembly preparatory process. The Holy Spirit-centred theme of the Canberra assembly remains a point of reference for ecumenical reflection, and a signpost for ecumenical vision.

3. The two following essays, *The First Vatican Council and the Petrine Office*, and *A Critical Assessment of Four Pro Oriente Consultations* discuss issues pertaining to Christology, primacy and conciliarity. These topics have again been moved to the fore of ecumenical debate, particularly in the context of bilateral dialogues.

9

4. The paper on *Unity and Mission in the Context of the Middle East* mainly deals with the inter-connectedness of unity and mission. Again, this is an old ecumenical debate that continues to get sharper focus from time to time in different regions and ecumenical situations.

5. *From Participation to Partnership* outlines, succinctly, the peculiar aspects of Orthodox witness in the ecumenical movement in general, and the WCC in particular. The contribution of Orthodoxy to ecumenism has always been a permanent concern for the Orthodox churches. The emergence of new ecumenical realities and tendencies has made them reassess the nature of their witness and the scope of their participation in the ecumenical movement.

6. The last article, namely *Towards a Self-Understanding of the World Council of Churches*, tackles some of the issues related to the common understanding of the nature and vocation of the WCC. This is a reflection process that was initiated some years ago by the Central Committee of the council. It will certainly become one of the pivotal concerns of the WCC in the years ahead.

While reading this book, it is important to bear certain points in mind. First, the papers collected under this cover are not scholarly presentations nor exhaustive accounts. They were prepared as lectures under special circumstances and for specific purposes. Hence, they are conditioned in terms of scope, approach and style. Secondly, the issues and themes wrestled with on the pages to follow are not of an academic nature, and are not treated as such. They are, as I have already pointed out, crucial issues that the Churches have been, in one way or another, grappling with in bilateral and multilateral theological dialogues as well as in their actual life and witness on local, regional and global levels. Most of the papers that appear in this book have already been published in different theological and ecumenical periodicals and reviews. In bringing them together I have made only a few editorial changes of minor importance.

The views and perspectives outlined on these pages are conveyed by someone who is called to serve the church of God in the Middle East, a region which, with its religious, cultural, social and political pluralism and tensions, provides a real challenge to Christian witness. The concerns and challenges displayed in this volume come from someone who is deeply rooted in his Oriental Orthodox tradition yet, at the same time, is open to other traditions, and strongly believes in dialogue among traditions. The ecumenical movement does not only promote dialogue and co-operation among the churches. It also makes them consciously aware of their dynamic interrelatedness in spite of their profound divisions. This book is a humble testimony to that creative and growing interrelatedness that I have learned and experienced in the ecumenical fellowship.

Before I conclude this introductory note, I would like to express my thanks to Dr Walter Arnold, a colleague in the Central Committee of the WCC who has written a foreword to this volume. I should say also a special word of thanks to the Oxford Centre for Mission Studies for publishing this book in its Regnum Books series.

Aram Keshishian
Beirut, Lebanon
January 1992

1

Justice, Peace and Creation, a Biblical Approach

A paper—here in its condensed form—read to a youth consultation on 'Justice, peace and integrity of creation' organized jointly by the youth departments of the European Conference of Churches and the Middle East Council of Churches, in Rome, June 1984.

The question of 'Justice, peace and integrity of creation' is a theological question *par excellence*, since it essentially deals with the God-human relationship. From a theological standpoint, justice, peace and creation are not different notions or independent realities, but interrelated aspects of one action, namely God's self-communication in time and space, and the human response to God's gift of life.

This essay aims to tackle JPIC in a biblical perspective. I consider the Bible the prime source of the issue under study. Therefore, any discussion of JPIC has to take into serious consideration the biblical concepts, insights and images. In this presentation I will spotlight, rather briefly, some of the major biblical dimensions and perspectives pertaining to justice, peace and creation. I will then make a few observations about their implications for the JPIC process.

Justice

JUSTICE IN THE OLD TESTAMENT

1. The Hebrew word for justice is *sedaga*. It is a common word in the Old Testament. What is particularly significant is that it frequently appears together with the terms salvation, fidelity, love and righteousness. These are closely interconnected in the theology of the Old Testament.

2. Justice is a theocentric reality. It is a gift of God, and not a human achievement. Justice belongs to God. It is the justice of God. In him justice is absolute and perfect: 'Just and right is he' (Deuteronomy 32:4)

3 Justice is not related to the external order. In other words, it cannot be defined as a fair distribution of power and material resources. Justice is God's commitment to his covenant, and the fidelity of humanity to it. Justice emerges from the faithful relationship of God and humanity, and manifests itself as love, righteousness and liberation in the life of God's people.

4. The justice of God is his mercy and love towards humankind. Therefore, it is not vindictive, but always salvific. Its intention is to liberate the human creature from the bondage of sin, slavery and oppression. It is significant to note that God remains faithful to his covenant even if it is rejected by his people. God is also a just and saving God in his wrath and punishment.

JUSTICE IN THE NEW TESTAMENT

1. The Greek term for justice is *dikaiosune*. In the New Testament, too, remarkably enough, justice is used in relation to, and sometimes equated with, promise, mercy, love and salvation.

2. God's justice is fully and concretely revealed in Christ. God and humanity were bound together in a covenantal bond. Human beings broke their side of the covenant by sin. God remained faithful to his covenant, and even merciful. God's intention was to give human beings a share in his divine justice so that they could remain in an eternal covenant with him through Jesus Christ.

3. Justice is not a state of being, but a way of doing. It is not merely keeping the law, but a right and obedient relationship with the Triune God in Christ, and a positive response to God's offer of life and salvation.

4. Justice is also a right relationship among human beings, with no discrimination between rich and poor, man and woman, Jew and Gentile. The vertical and horizontal dimensions of justice are inseparably interwoven. They condition each other. This is at the heart of the New Testament understanding of justice.

CONCLUSION

In conclusion, in both Old and New Testaments justice is theo-centric. It is integral to God's nature and revelation. Justice is manifested through God's fidelity to his promise of salvation despite human sin and infidelity. God's justice is based on mercy and love. He rebukes injustice and fights against unjust social orders, but he never breaks his covenant with his people. Justice is righteousness—that is being on the way of God. Therefore, it is not something to be achieved, but something to be accepted by human beings as a gift of God, and to be implemented in total obedience to and dependence upon God.

Peace

PEACE IN THE OLD TESTAMENT

1. The Hebrew word for peace is *shalom*. It comes from the root *slm* which means to be complete, whole. Peace refers to an ideal state of life untouched by violence or disorder, and sustained by security, prosperity and good relationships between persons and nations (2 Kings 20:19; Psalm 37:11; Isaiah 32:18).

2. Peace comes only from God who is the source of peace in all its forms and manifestations (Judges 6:24; Isaiah 45:7). Only God overcomes the forces of evil (Job 25:2), and establishes peace.

3. The covenant that God has made with humanity is a covenant of peace (Ezekiel 34:25; Isaiah 54:10; Jeremiah 29:11), since it aims at the restoration of the relationship of humanity with God. In spite of the human rejection of peace, God always desires peace to human-ity: 'My covenant of peace shall not be removed' (Isaiah 54:10).

4. Peace is identified with liberation, particularly in prophecies. In fact, the coming of the Messiah is the coming of the Prince of Peace (Isaiah 9:6), God's liberator, who will abolish wars and violence, will deliver God's people from their enemies, and establish peace and justice on earth. The whole of prophetic literature is, indeed, a cry for peace, (Jeremiah 33:6; Isaiah 55:12). God's peace is, there-fore, his liberation (Isaiah 52:7). Those who trust him are liberated, and are in peace.

5. Peace and justice are intimately interrelated. Peace is not only the

well-being of human beings in both the physical and the spiritual sense, but fundamentally their obedient relationship with God. It is the righteousness of humanity under the covenant. To be at peace means to be upright and faithful (Malachi 2:6). In other terms, peace is conditioned by justice. It means to practise justice (Isaiah 59:8).

PEACE IN THE NEW TESTAMENT

1. Peace is equivalent to *eirene* in Greek which means salvation, reconciliation with God, victory over evil (Romans 5:1; Colossians 1:20) and right relations among human beings. Peace is the fullness of the divine gift of salvation in Christ.

2. God is the God of peace (Romans 15:33). The coming of God's kingdom in Christ is the coming of God's peace: 'Glory to God in the highest, and on earth peace' (Luke 2:14). Christ's life, death and resurrection are God's gospel of peace for the whole world (Acts 10:36).

3. Not only is Christ the messenger of peace (Matthew 5:9), he himself makes God's peace actual in human history. Peace is given to the world as life to be lived, as a mission to be accomplished: 'My peace I give to you... in me you may have peace' (John 14:27; 16:33). Peace as God's gift of life in Jesus Christ to humanity and creation includes four vital dimensions:

First, it is the reconciliation of humanity with God. The old nature has distorted its *imago Dei*; it was 'alienated' from God (Ephesians 4:18) and has become an 'enemy' of God (Romans 5:10). In Christ humanity was reconciled to God, and has 'peace with God through our Lord Jesus Christ' (Romans 5:1). God by his own initiative has made peace with humanity through the cross (Colossians 1:20).

Secondly, peace is eternal life in contrast to the sinful life which leads to death (Romans 8:6–11). Peace is the rejection of sin and life dominated by evil, and acceptance of 'abundant life' in Christ.

Thirdly, peace is harmonious relations between nations and the removal of all sorts of injustice and discrimination between people (Acts 2:6; 1 Corinthians 7:15; Ephesians 2:14–17; Mark 9:50).

Fourthly, peace does not only imply a just inter-human relationship, but also harmony with God's creation. In fact, to be in a good relationship with God implies being in a good relationship with God's creation.

4. Peace is not only an eschatological reality, but a present reality

here and now. It is a given reality in Christ. The incarnate God himself became the peace of the world (Ephesians 2:14). Whoever is in Christ is in peace; whoever participates in God's peace through Christ is called to live out that peace and be its messenger.

CONCLUSION

In conclusion, peace in biblical understanding is not a human-made reality. It is God's life, justice and liberation offered to humanity and the whole creation. Christ is the actualization of peace. He remains the only peace of the world, his cross the way of peace, and the resurrection the victory of peace. Those who say 'yes' to Christ are in peace. Those who reject him are in death.

Creation

CREATION IN THE OLD TESTAMENT

1. Creation is the beginning of God's revelation, and the starting point of history. God created the cosmos *ex nihilo*. The creative work of God also included the processes which formed the universe.

2. God's creation is characterized by relationship, order and unity. All creatures are necessarily in relationship with their creator. The relationship of irrational creatures with God is one of sheer dependence and contingency, and that of rational beings is one of obedient response.

Within the created order each creature fulfills the creator's will. Each creature has a specific task. Human beings have a peculiar place and a special role in creation. Their answerability to God implies special responsibility towards creation. Created in the image of their creator, human beings are called to act as the representatives of God. They are the administrators of God's work (Genesis 1:28), his co-workers. They must exercise sovereignty within God's sovereignty.

Unity in diversity is a salient feature of creation. All creatures are an integral part of a diversified yet interdependent whole. The wholeness and integrity of creation are safeguarded by responsible human stewardship.

3. Creation is not an arbitrary act of God. It is the expression of God's love and freedom. Nor is creation an aimless self-sufficient

existence. It is the beginning of God's covenant with humanity. It provides the setting within which God's saving work takes place. Therefore, creation has no existence apart from God, and no meaning apart from humanity. Creation is the beginning of God's *economia*. In fact, creation and redemption are interrelated dimensions of salvation history. It is important to emphasize that first, God's providence is extended beyond the individual person to the whole of humanity, history and creation. It a has cosmic dimension. Secondly, God's salvific act is not confined to, nor absorbed in time. It takes place in time and space, yet it transcends time limits. It is God's eternal creating and sustaining act. God is present in his creation and is in permanent relationship with it.

4. God is not identified with his creation; he is immanent yet transcendent. This implies two things. First, although creation is an accomplished fact, it is, at the same time, continuously being created—that is in the process of becoming. Secondly, God does not limit himself to conserving his creation. He constantly renews and protects it by his providence.

5. The universe was created to be 'good' (Genesis 1:31). The Good cannot create but good. Creation is an act of goodness. Its intention is for the good of human beings. Evil is not part of creation. It is the negation of creation. However, evil, in various forms and manifestations, exists in creation. It is the rebellion of humanity against the creator. It is a threat to creation. Old Testament theology rejects the ultimate dualism of good and evil. The latter is the absence of good, and eventually will be conquered by good.

CREATION IN THE NEW TESTAMENT

1. The New Testament speaks of new creation. In Christ is found the new creation (2 Corinthians 5:17; Ephesians 2:10). He is the inaugurator of the new covenant, and the relation of God's purpose for the world (Ephesians 1:9–10). In Christ all things are made new, all things 'hold together' (Colossians 1:17). Through him and in the power of the Holy Spirit God constantly creates, upholds and redeems creation in its wholeness.

2. Creation is fallen due to original sin. It groans under the bondage of corruption. The purpose of God's incarnation was the re-creation of creation. Re-creation is the salvation and liberation of both humanity and creation from sin, evil and death. In Christ God won

the victory over corruption, disintegration and death, and initiated a new creation and a new humanity. In Christ humanity and creation entered into new relationship with God: 'If any one is in Christ, he is a new creation; the old has passed away, behold, the new has come' (2 Corinthians 5:17). However, human beings are, at every moment, falling by putting themselves at the centre of creation. But God is eternally creator and redeemer. Out of his love and mercy God is eternally re-creating and renewing humanity and creation.

3. Hence, in Christ the new creation has already become a reality. The *eschaton* (the Last Days) became present. But the full disclosure of the new creation lies in God's future, where his kingdom will be fully realized and 'the new heaven and the new earth', free from corruption, evil and death, will appear (Isaiah 66:22; Revelation 21:1–4). Humanity, creation and history are oriented towards a definite purpose: the kingdom of God.

CONCLUSION

In sum, it is important to stress that biblical theology rejects pantheistic, emanationistic and dualistic theories of creation. Creation is the free act of God. It is God's gift of love and life. God created the world to be a dwelling place (Isaiah 45:18). He stands in personal relationship with his creation. The latter is not an anthropocentric nor a self-sustaining reality; it is totally dependent on its creator. Creation is not a self-centered entity. Its aim is beyond itself. Creation is not an endlessly becoming reality either. It has a definite goal towards which it moves. In the Old Testament creation has to be seen in the context of the covenant. In the New Testament it must be viewed Christologically. In both creation has a soteriological meaning and purpose. In Christ corrupted creation was remade, fallen humanity was re-established. Human beings are called to be God's co-workers and servants participating in full obedience in God's work of re-creation in Christ.

A few observations

After this sketchy presentation of the biblical view of justice, peace and creation, I would like to raise two questions: What is the responsibility of humankind towards justice, peace and creation? What are the implications of biblical teachings to the JPIC process? Let me make a few observations:

1. Justice, peace and creation are God-given responsibilities. They essentially belong to God. They are an integral part of God's revelation. Human beings can neither possess them nor can they impose their will on them. They are given for the good of humanity, for the salvation of the world, and ultimately for the kingdom of God. Humankind has a special responsibility, the God-given stewardship to be the custodian of creation, the messenger of peace and the fulfiller of justice. They are not the rights but, rather, the obligations of humankind.

2. Justice, peace and creation have to be seen in the perspective of the kingdom of God. They are the concrete manifestations of God's redemptive work as well as the foretaste and promise of the eschatological fulfilment of the kingdom. They are acts of grace when we respond to them positively. But they become acts of judgment when we reject them and practise injustice, violence and exploitation. The history of the Old Testament is an eloquent example in this respect. In fact, all human-centred forces eventually become oppressive and destructive, and human-made systems false absolutes, if they do not serve the promotion of justice, peace and integrity of creation, namely, the kingdom of God.

3. Justice, peace and creation are the fruits of the reconciliation of humanity with God. Apart from God the *imago Dei* of humankind is fallen, justice is diverted, peace disappears, and creation is distorted. Justice, peace and integrity of creation are being authenticated and maintained intact and strong only in communion with the Triune God. Christ is the reconciler between humanity and God. Therefore, being 'in Christ' (2 Corinthians 5:17) is being in reconciliation with God which, in turn, implies practising justice, working for peace and being concerned with the integrity and sustainability of creation.

4. Christian theology rejects any kind of separation between justice and peace. They are inseparably and dynamically interwoven. They condition and strengthen each other. It is simply heresy to speak in the name of peace and practise injustice. Peace is not the absence of war. It is a state of being where people's right to self-determination and a dignified life are fully respected. Lasting and genuine peace is based on justice—that is equality, mutual love, co-responsibility and accountability.

5. There exists a creative interrelation between God, humanity and creation. Western theology introduced a dichotomy between God,

humanity and creation. Humanity and creation are two estranged entities that oppose each other: for the sake of human progress creation must be conquered and exploited. In contrast, Orthodox theology continues to maintain a dynamic unity between humanity and creation. Humanity is part of all creation, and all creation is part of humanity. The latter is shaped by creation, and, in turn, humanity is called to shape and re-shape it. There exists an inner relatedness between the two. Creation is not a divinized reality; yet it has its proper place and dignity in God's plan for the kingdom.

Human beings have no right to exploit creation for their own ends. Pollution and exploitation of the natural environment are against the plan of God. Astronomy, geology, ecology, biology and other natural sciences undoubtedly opened new dimensions in human knowledge of creation. They challenged the accepted norms, beliefs and theories. But however equipped with new discoveries, humankind cannot claim to be the absolute owner, the freeholder of creation. Humanity remains God's steward, called to cultivate, nurture and protect the integrity of creation. This means that human beings are not purely guardians. They are rational beings with a sense of responsibility and a God-given vocation. God and human beings are partners, co-workers. The latter cannot master the world by themselves and for themselves. They are always accountable to God.

The role of the World Council of Churches

The sixth assembly of the World Council of Churches in Vancouver in 1983 asked the council 'to engage the member churches in a conciliar process of mutual commitment (covenant) to justice, peace and the integrity of creation.' The issues of justice, peace and integrity of creation were not new for the WCC. They had been major impulses and concerns in the formation of the WCC and the development of ecumenical social thought. What was of special importance with the Vancouver call was that vis-à-vis the growing awareness of a global crisis, it emphasized the interrelatedness of justice, peace and integrity of creation and, as such, it made an urgent appeal for a united struggle to face the new threats. The World Council took the call of Vancouver seriously with the profound conviction that the new understanding of, and renewed commitment to justice, peace and integrity of creation will re-orient its priorities.

As a sign of its commitment the WCC established a special programme under the name of 'Justice, peace and integrity of creation' (briefly known as JPIC) with a task of discussing what is already happening in different situations and in different parts of the world, and gathering them together for a comprehensive ecumenical response. To this end, and with the active participation of the Roman Catholic Church and non-member churches, national and regional ecumenical organizations, youth movements and action groups, a number of national, regional and international consultations were held and a series of resource materials were published dealing from different perspectives with various aspects and dimensions of the issue. The JPIC World Convocation in Seoul (5–12 March 1990) is a comprehensive exposition of the various manifestations of the issue as well as reaffirmation of ecumenical concerns for, and involvement in the struggle for justice, peace and integrity of creation. As the Central Committee of the WCC stated, this ecumenical commitment will stay 'at the heart of the ecumenical vision for the next millennium'.

2

Justice, Peace and Integrity of Creation in a Eucharistic Perspective

A lecture given to an international consultation on 'Justice, peace and integrity of creation' convened by the WCC in Glion, Switzerland, 6–13 November, 1985.

It is important to state at the very outset of this paper that 'Justice, peace and integrity of creation', as a process of reflection and action, is intimately related to the nature of the church and its mission. Therefore the ecclesiological dimension must be taken seriously into consideration as we attempt to identify the specific nature and the scope of the churches' commitment to the process referred to.

My task is, as I understand it, to look at eucharist as one of the basic ecclesial forms and powerful ways of the church's involvement in JPIC. I will, first, bring under focus those characteristic aspects of the eucharist which have, in my judgment, significant bearing on the subject under consideration. Secondly, I will underscore the missiological importance of eucharist. Thirdly, I will briefly spell out some of the implications of eucharist for JPIC. I would like to remind you that I will be treating the subject as an Orthodox. As you know the Orthodox attach a particular importance to eucharist in the life and mission of the church. Eucharist has a unique place and a pivotal role in Orthodox theology.

Some significant aspects of eucharist

It is not my intention to deal with the eucharist *per se*. I will identify only those dimensions of eucharist which have immediate relevance to the JPIC process.

EUCHARIST: THE FOCUS OF THE CHURCH

The church is a eucharistic community. The eucharist constitutes the church. The church is never conceived in terms of its geographical boundaries, institutional structures and hierarchical orders. This is, indeed, a false ecclesiology. The church of God that we have been discussing in this consultation—whether it is described in terms of 'universal church', 'local church', 'confessing church', 'prophetic church', 'church of the covenant', 'church of the poor', 'people's church', or whatever—is the local community gathered around the eucharist. In the eucharist the church becomes what it ought to become—that is the recreated cosmos, the *koinonia* in the Triune God, the anticipation of the kingdom of God.

The eucharist displays five major dimensions. The eucharist is:

1. thanksgiving to the Father for his continuous redemption and sanctification of the whole creation;

2. the anamnesis of God's reconciling act in Christ;

3. the foretaste of Christ's *parousia*, and the fulfilment of the kingdom;

4. the *epiklesis*—that is, the church's prayer for the Spirit to sanctify and empower it to fulfill its mission in the world;

5. a *koinonia*—that is communion in a twofold sense: participation in the body of Christ, and the community of those who participate in Christ's body.[1]

Hence, eucharist is not just a 'sacrament', but the mystery of our participation in the life of the Triune God. It is also the locus of God's continuous recreation and sanctification of creation, and the living presence of the kingdom.

EUCHARIST: THE SOURCE OF CATHOLICITY

Catholicity in its profound theological sense is the wholeness and fullness of God's act of recreating, saving and restoring humanity and creation into their original being. It is existentially experienced and concretely expressed in and through the eucharist which is the source and the sign of true catholicity. The eucharist is, in fact, the 'catholic act' of the 'catholic church'—that is, the local church. Through eucharist the church lives out its fullness and wholeness, namely its catholicity. The local church offers the eucharist on behalf of the whole church and creation. By virtue of its catholicity the eucharist comprises all the members of the church in a given locality irrespective of sex, age or race. It also embraces the whole church of God in all its fullness in all places and times as well as the whole created cosmos. The local eucharistic community is, therefore, not a part of the catholic church, but the catholic church itself. Through the eucharist a local church transcends its national, social, ethnic and geographical boundaries, and enters into communion with all other local churches.

The catholicity of the church is not confined to the eucharist. It is ultimately an eschatological reality. Its nature is revealed and experienced here and now in the celebration of eucharist. One may rightly speak of the eucharistic nature of the catholicity and the catholic nature of the eucharist.[2]

EUCHARIST: THE GIFT OF LIFE

Life is at the heart of the eucharist. To this effect five points deserve our attention. The eucharist is:

1. the source of authentic life, namely, God's gift of life to human beings and creation;

2. the feast of life, the celebration of the wholeness of created life;

3. thanksgiving to God for his gift of life in Christ;

4. participation in the life of the Triune God;

5. sanctification of the whole of life in all its dimensions and expressions.

Life given by God to human beings is not only a physical existence. It is the self-communication of God in sacrificial love in Jesus Christ to his creation. In the eucharist Christ is proclaimed as the only life of the world (John 6:47–57). This life is a life of salvation and liberation, renewal and hope, justice and peace which is constantly celebrated in, and offered through, the eucharist as the true life of humanity and the whole creation. The eucharist is, therefore, the penetration of the 'abundant life' into the corrupted life and its re-creation. Through the eucharist broken human lives are restored, human beings are rescued from sin and death and given eternal life, and the whole creation is renewed and transformed. In other terms, in the eucharist the whole of life in all its forms and manifestations is redeemed and sanctified, and set on the way towards *theosis*. In fact, the eucharist is the celebration of new life in Christ. The incarnate God 'conquered death by death' (Armenian liturgy), and became the life of the world. Human life is lifeless without the eucharistic dimension and vision.

24

EUCHARIST: THE LOCUS OF UNITY

The eucharist is the focal point and the supreme moment of God-human dialogue. Through it God becomes with us (Emmanuel), and for the whole creation. The eucharist is, *par excellence*, the sacrament of unity in a twofold sense:

1. the unity between Christ and his people as well as among the people who constitute the *koinonia* is fully revealed and existentially experienced through the sharing of bread and wine;

2. in a local eucharistic gathering all believers of all places and times are united in one and the same fellowship: 'Because there is one bread, we who are many are one body, for we all partake of the one bread' (1 Corinthians 10:17).

The eucharist is the sacramental encounter and a new covenant between God and humanity. In it, humanity and creation are reconciled with God, and are renewed and sanctified, and restored in their true image and vocation. A reconciled diversity of men and women, white and black, poor and rich, time and space, past, present and future is brought about in the eucharist, making it the sign and instrument of the reconciliation and transformation of the whole creation.

EUCHARIST: THE FORETASTE OF THE KINGDOM

As I pointed out earlier, in the eucharist the church becomes what it is called to become—the anticipation of the kingdom. The latter constitutes the very nature and the goal of the eucharist. In the celebration of the eucharist the church receives the gift of the kingdom through the sacrifice of Christ and becomes the foretaste of the kingdom. The eucharist is, in fact, the church becoming the kingdom of God. Hence, the eucharist is more than the proclamation of the kingdom. By making the Christ-event a living reality in the life of the community, the eucharist actualizes the kingdom of God which becomes a reality 'here and now' and, at the same time, 'not yet'. The eucharist orients the worshipping community towards the actual world, and, at the same time, towards the *eschaton* (Last Days). The eucharist actualizes a continuous *parousia* (return of Christ), a realized *eschaton*. That which belongs to the past and to the eschaton makes us live here and now. This is a vital dimension of Orthodox eucharist.

EUCHARIST: THE RE-CREATED CREATION

The eucharist embraces not only the whole of Christ's body in time and space, but also the whole of humanity and the entire creation. Humanity and creation, history and eschatology, time and space are incorporated and inseparably united in the eucharist. Therefore, the eucharist is not offered only on behalf of and for the church, but on behalf of and for the whole creation. In it the church prays for the sanctification of the entire creation. Through it the created order is re-created and restored to its fullness, wholeness, integrity and authenticity.

It is important to emphasize that the church and creation eschatologically belong together. It is wrong, therefore, to draw a line of demarcation between the church and creation, the sacred and profane. 'All things' are created and sustained by God. There is no dualism and dichotomy between creation and the eucharistic community. The whole of life and the whole of creation are sacred and remain within God's sight. The church and creation are not self-sufficient entities; they are for the kingdom. They have to be seen in the perspective of the eucharist. There is no 'world's agenda' and 'church's agenda'. There is only God's agenda for the kingdom. The Christian's heavenly citizenship (Hebrews 13:14) does not put him over against the world. Rather it sends him to the world to transform it. This is the basic theme in Orthodox theology and spirituality.

Eucharist and mission

Eucharist is essentially a missionary event. It is not a ceremonial festival as it is sometimes wrongly referred to. The eucharistic nature of mission and the missionary dimension of eucharist have to be spelled out more dynamically.

1. The eucharist brings about a double openness—communion in the Triune God and participation in the healing and saving work of God in and for the world. These vertical and horizontal dimensions of eucharist are interrelated. The eucharistic experience of renewal, reconciliation and *theosis* ought to be lived out in the world and for the world. The crucified and risen Christ has to be taken to the world as the life of the world. The eucharistic community does not exist for itself, but for the world. It is called to reincarnate the eucharist in all its dimensions and implications in the actual life of society, becoming the living witness of the victory of life over death,

love over hatred, justice over injustice, reconciliation over separation.

2. The eucharistic openness to the world is not a blind identification of the church with the world. It is a full, active and conscious participation in God's ongoing work of renewal, reconciliation and transformation of humanity and creation. Through the eucharist human beings are restored in their God-given responsibility to be 'co-workers' with God. This means that:

a.   the mission of the church is rooted in, and emerges from the eucharist;

b.   the eucharist is not just anamnesis, namely the remembrance of God's saving act in Christ, but fundamentally a sharing of God's love and promise, liberation and salvation with human beings, and a restoring of the brokenness of humanity and the integrity of creation.

Therefore mission, in its genuine sense, is eucharist in extension.

3. Eucharist and mission are not two independent functions of the church, but two interdependent manifestations of one action aimed at building up the kingdom of God. As indicated earlier, eucharist without outreach is just a memorial service; and mission without a eucharistic dimension and vision lacks any ecclesial nature. The eucharist is not a sacramental act of the church by which it only remembers and waits. It is fundamentally the action of the church by which it grows in communion with God, and participates in the Christ-event for the salvation of the world. The eucharist empowers the community of faith to live with Christ, to suffer with Christ and witness to Christ in deed and in word. Therefore, the eucharist is both the ingoing and the outgoing of the church, the church's becoming kingdom in time and space.

4. The eucharist is not a self-contained action of the church detached from the world and worldly things. It transcends time and geographical limits and limitations, and sends the church to the world. In fact, the eucharist does not come to an end with the final blessing 'Go forth in peace.' In a sense, it starts with it, and continues, in different forms and ways, in the world. This is what is usually referred to in Orthodox theology as 'liturgy after liturgy'. The church does not become a eucharistic community only around the Lord's table. It is always and everywhere a eucharistic community— that is a eucharist-centered and eucharist-oriented community. The

church cannot exist and witness without the eucharist. The eucharist is the ground of the church's existence, the mystery of its inner growth, and the source of its missionary outgoing.

5. The outgoing of the eucharistic community must not be understood in quantitative, but rather in qualitative terms. It makes Christ a living reality in the world, and the saving and liberating power of the world. The eucharistic community is not a spectator in the world. It is sent to the world with a special mission—to become a confessing, witnessing and struggling community in the midst of injustice, oppression and alienation. Having been deified through the eucharist the eucharistic community is called to announce the good news to the poor by liberating the captives from oppressive structures, by bearing witness to God's truth and love, by struggling for justice, peace and inviolability of life, by living the kingdom of God in all its demands and implications.

6. The eucharist is the sacrament of suffering and of overcoming, overcoming in suffering. The proclamation of the lordship of Christ is not a triumphalistic act, but a real *kenosis*. The extension of eucharist in time and space is not an easy process but a sacrificial one, since it is never compassion or aid but total identification with the world's suffering and pain in self-giving love. It is a confrontation with the evils and 'principalities' of the world and 'the powers of darkness' (Ephesians 6:12). It is a continuous struggle against an unjust *status quo*. It is *marturia* in life even in death. In fact, communion in the death and resurrection of Christ impells the eucharistic community to share that joy with the poor, sick, oppressed and marginalized. The eucharistic anticipation of the kingdom of God makes the community of faith not only a partner, but the avant-garde of the struggle for a just society, a peaceful world, reconciled humanity and sustainable creation. Hence, the commitment of the eucharistic community to 'Justice, peace and integrity of creation' springs from the sacramental communion in the death and resurrection of Christ: 'The kingdom of God is not food and drink, but righteousness and peace and joy' (Romans 14:17).

7. In the eucharist two interrelated movements take place at the same time: gathering and sending forth in the name of Jesus Christ. The mission of the church must flow from the eucharist, and come back to it as the locus of the real presence of God's coming kingdom,

the source of God's eternal life given in Christ, and the *ekklesia* becoming the recreated cosmos. The eucharist is the continuous reincarnation of Christ in the world. It determines and sustains the church's presence and witness in the world. The church must never lose the eucharistic vision of its mission, and the incarnational nature of the eucharist. The eucharist is the 'first fruits' of the new creation offered for the renewal and transformation of the whole creation. It is a living and continuous reminder addressed to the world that 'the time is fulfilled and the kingdom of God is at hand; repent, and believe in the gospel' (Mark 1:15). Eucharist is a grace and an invitation, a promise and a challenge.

Eucharist and JPIC

With such an understanding of the nature and the meaning of eucharist, one may safely state that the eucharistic dimension is crucial for JPIC. Any further elaboration of this basic ecclesiological stand is beyond the purview of this paper. As we embark on the JPIC process, I believe that it is a major task for the WCC to invite the churches to translate, in concrete terms and in their own ways and situations, their eucharistic experience and vision into a common commitment to JPIC. I would like, by way of summary, to single out some of the implications of eucharist to the JPIC process:

1. The eucharist is the celebration and actualization of the victory of life over death; the reconciliation of humanity with God; the restoration of justice and peace on the earth; the anticipation of the kingdom of God; and the re-creation of the whole creation in Christ. What does it mean, in concrete ways, to participate in the eucharist and live it out in and for the world?

2. The eucharistic community is a confessing and witnessing community sent to the world for the transformation and sanctification of creation. It is neither the master of, nor an observer in creation. It is a partner in the renewing, liberating and sanctifying work of God. What are the implications of this partnership in terms of commitment to the conciliar process of 'Justice, peace and integrity of creation'?

3. The interconnectedness of justice, peace and life is dynamically manifested in the eucharist (Romans 14:17; 1 Corinthians 11:20–23; 2 Corinthians 8:14). Threats to peace are threats to justice and

life, and the other way around. How can the churches, in a holistic approach, express, in their life and witness, the indivisibility of justice, peace and life, as well as constantly remind the world of their sacredness as God-given gifts and a responsibility to human-kind?

4. Life belongs to God. He is the only source, guarantee and goal of life. Therefore, life is never the possession of human beings. It is given to them to protect and enrich it, and offer it for the glory of God. Any threat against life irrespective of its origin, nature or purpose is a defiance of God. A comprehensive and theological understanding of life is crucial. This question must be given a special attention in the JPIC process.

Notes

1. It is significant to note that the well-known consensus document of the WCC, namely, *Baptism, Eucharist and Ministry*, commonly known as BEM, has given a special importance to these dimensions of the eucharist.

2. I have more extensively treated the eucharist as the source of catholicity and unity in my book *Conciliar Fellowship: A Common Goal*, WCC, 1992.

3

Human Beings in Creation

*A lecture delivered to the consultation on
'Tradition and Renewal in Orthodox
Education' held in Bucharest, Romania, 6–12
September, 1976.[1]*

In the present age of advanced technology, human beings hardly look at themselves with an attempt to re-examine who they are and re-assess their individual vocations in the created order. Their eyes are directed towards the discovery of new planets. Their minds are being focussed on new ventures in the realm of science and technology. It is a fact now that many of the 'mysteries' of creation have been largely disclosed. The unknown has, to a considerable degree, become known. More than at any time in history, human beings master creation. Creation has become anthropocentric.

In spite of enormous achievements and advances in almost all spheres of human life, the perennial question remains as valid and crucial as ever: who and what is a human being? In fact, human beings still remain unknown to themselves, a question to themselves (Augustine). They realize that they cannot find themselves in themselves (Pascal); they need to transcend themselves in order to understand and fulfil themselves. In this century of miraculous discoveries, the human being remains an undiscovered mystery. In the words of A. Carell, *'L'homme c'est inconnu'*.

Neither the space allowed, nor the scope of the consultation permit me to grapple with this pertinent question in all its dimensions. The focal aim of this paper is to outline the Christian view of humanity in its major aspects and with particular reference to the role of human beings in creation.

Views on humanity

The self-understanding of human beings has been a permanent concern and endeavour from the remotest times of human history. Ancient Greek philosophy conceived human beings as being the only creatures who have the *logos* (Plato). They are rational animals (Aristotle). The so-called *logos* concept prevailed for many centuries, becoming a central trend of Christian anthropology which considered *divinum* as the source of *humanum*.

Religious anthropology generally considers a human being to be a macrocosm who unites the material and the spiritual words which are in continuous tension. Human beings are motivated by internal drives for the search for the supernatural. They are not merely what they are, what they appear to be. Their existence is measured by something higher than themselves. In fact, the quest for transcendence is at the heart of religious anthropology.

With the advance of science and technology, and the increase of interreligious and interracial relations, biological, cultural, social, political and other anthropologies were developed. They explored new dimensions of human nature.

In political and social anthropologies, human beings are perceived functionally. They are 'social animals', inseparably related to a given socio-political milieu. Human beings are what they make of themselves. They are both the producer and the product of their work (Marx), which determines their nature, and measures their value politically, socially and economically.

For psychology, the nervous system is the source of energy. It sustains the human physical existence. Its various activities such as doubt, despair, anxiety, love, sexual desire, and so on, together constitute the human nature. Biology defines human beings genetically. They are bundles of biological impulses.

One may gather these and several other views in two ideological categories: idealism and materialism. Idealism starts from reason and attempts to explain all human dynamics as derivative from it. The material nature of human beings is regarded as an accident which does not concern their essential being. Materialism identifies the real essence of human beings in their material nature; reason is only an epiphenomenon of the material life. The plain fact is that the extensive research into the biological origins of humanity (Darwin), the concept of environmental determinism (Marx), the self-sufficiency of reason (Hegel), the assertion of self-certainty (Descartes), the discovery of the importance of moral consciousness (Kant), the development of I-Thou interdependent existence (Buber), and similar concepts have failed to provide a comprehensive view of the real nature and true image of a human being. Their findings remain partial and unsatisfactory, ambiguous and confusing, although Christian anthropology may use many of their insights.

The biblical view

A scrutinizing textual and theological inquiry into key biblical terms such as flesh, body, soul, heart and breath reveal the basic thrusts of Old Testament anthropology. I would like to draw your attention only to some of the most significant aspects of the biblical view of human beings and their specific status in creation and vis-à-vis God.

According to the creation story, which constitutes the ground of biblical anthropology, human existence is due to an act of divine free will. We learn from the same story that the first man is created in the 'image' and 'likeness' of God. In fact, the *imago Dei* is the core of humanity's *humanitas*, and constitutes its distinctive mark. It basically shows itself in human rationality, responsible freedom and answerability to God. The image of God is not an actuality, but a possibility. It is a divine gift for a responsible and God-centred life. Human nature is not something static, but dynamic—in the process of becoming in the 'likeness' of God. The human creature stands at the centre of creation, and is given the task to rule over it, to be God's co-creator and covenant partner. Human beings totally and irrevocably find their fullness, authentic humanness and salvation only in fellowship with God. This ontological interrelation between the creator and the creature determines and conditions the very being of the creature. Therefore, human beings are a theological reality; their existence is a theological one.

The God-human dialogue is actual, concrete. It takes place in history, in community. Human beings are given the gift of being able to receive God's revelation, and respond to it. They may also reject God's gift of life, subjecting themselves to sin and death. Thus, human existence is in tension. There is a continuous conflict between the divine determination and human self-determination. There is a dialectical interaction between growing in the image of God, and the prevailing fallen state of humanity. A human being is constantly exposed to glory and life, on the one hand, and to self-centredness and death, on the other.

The teaching of the Old Testament is that:

1. The call of God does not cease even if human hearing is perverted.

2. Human self-understanding takes place only in the context of divine self-communication.

3. God and humanity are inseparably inter-related. God is God-for-humanity, humanity is humanity-for-God.

Old Testament anthropology is fundamentally a theo-anthropology.

New Testament anthropology is Christocentric anthropology. The *imago Dei* was fulfilled, fallen humanity was restored and authentic humanity was revealed in Jesus Christ. God in Christ became a partaker in human nature to liberate human beings from their sinful state. Adam was created in the image of God; the New Adam became the *eikon* of God (Colossians 1:15–18), the living and operating presence of God in the world. Jesus Christ is God *in exinantio*, and man *in exaltatio*, the way of God's 'downward to man', and 'man's upward to God' (Barth). He is the locus where God's intended humanity for human being was focused, where the meaning and the essential quality of human existence was actualized. Hence, 'Behold the man' (John 19:5), the *vere homo*, in whom the Triune God not only disclosed his being and gave himself, but also provided human beings with the knowledge of himself becoming 'the answer to man's question about himself' (Moltmann). 'Behold the man' who became the prototype of authentic humanness, and 'the way' leading to fellowship with God.

As a human being Jesus Christ is like us, but in his true humanity, he is unlike us. He is the lamb slain for the re-humanization of humanity and transformation of creation, and their reconciliation with God. Through the reconciling work of Christ, humankind was given a new 'courage to be' (Tillich), a new vision to face the future responsibly and in freedom. He is both the object of God's free and liberating grace, and the subject in whom the human creature was renewed and reconciled with the creator. In other words, in Christ 'the elected man' and 'the electing God' (Barth) came together. In him God became man in order that human beings might become God (Athanasius)—fully and authentically themselves. Therefore, this God-man is God-with-us (Immanuel), and God-for-us.

His action is his action for us. His knowledge includes human knowledge of himself. His history is our history. In his humanity our human nature was exalted and our existence received new meaning and orientation. By his cross, conflict with God was turned into peace, alienation into fellowship, rejection into obedience, slavery into freedom. Jesus Christ is the *arche* and *eschaton* (Revelation

1:17; 22:13) of true and free humanity. The event of the Word-made-flesh has ontological significance. It is addressed to human beings in all their internal dimensions and external structures and relationships. It has also cosmic implications. In the incarnation the whole created order was transfigured, and a new creation has been inaugurated. The Christ-event is an actualized fact once and for all. It is, at the same time, in the process of becoming through the church, the body of Christ.

Jesus Christ is a historical reality, yet, at the same time, an eschatological reality. Both poles of his existence sustain human life and give it the hope to look beyond the present to Christ's second coming in the *parousia*. The Christian doctrine of humanity is not a theory, but a confession of faith grounded on a historical event. Christian understanding of humanity does not emerge from an empirical analysis or philosophical reflection, but from the living encounter of humanity with God in Jesus Christ. For Christian anthropology the real human being is Jesus Christ, 'the man for the other' (Barth). 'Being in Christ' (Paul) is the only way of being authentically human. The human creature may be 'far' from God. But God is 'not far from each one of us', 'in him we live and move and have our being' (Acts 17:27–28). 'Being in Christ' means being for others, sharing ourselves with others. It also implies being in the process of 'becoming man' (Baum). In fact, human beings must fulfill their humanity as a divine gift and task.

Humanity in a secularized world

The world of the twentieth century is in rapid and radical change. The impact of enormous changes is experienced in almost all domains of society and life. The challenge of secularization and technology is always strong and crucial. The present century is marked by the domination of the secular over the sacred, of science over religion, of technology over metaphysics.

The life of contemporary societies is characterized by strong pragmatism and empiricism. The experiment has become the test of truth. In a world of growing desacralization human beings have acquired a new image, a new understanding of history and their role. They have created their own structures of meaning and value systems; they themselves have become the norm. The domain enlightened by God's revealed truth is being overshadowed by the spheres conquered by human power.

The gradual dominance of empiricism and secularism has prepared the ground for the 'eclipse of God' (Buber). We often hear the voice of Nietzsche: 'God is dead'. In fact, a new vision of God is dawning upon the horizon of the 'secular city' (Cox); a new experience of God is emerging in technologically oriented societies. The religious premises of the ancient world are not longer valid for the human being who has 'come of age' (Bonhoeffer).

Modern men and women understand themselves as belonging totally to the flux of secular history, to the industrialized society, to the anthropocentric creation. They believe what they know experimentally. The spiritual dimension of their lives has been overshadowed by mundane interests. The possibilities of relating themselves in hope to any transcendental reality have considerably been decreased. All these facts point to the growing trend of what is termed secular humanism which affirms humanity without God, obscures the vision of the kingdom of God, and leads humanity to self-confidence and self-deification. Therefore, secular humanism in all its ideological aspects and institutional manifestations has to be rejected as a dehumanizing force in human society.

Technology, which used to be considered an indispensable tool for the creation of a better world, has become an oppressive and dehumanizing factor. It must be controlled and undergirded by a value-system that generates justice and equal sharing of power. Humanity is in urgent need of humanization and liberation from the self-certainty that alienates it from God and creation. History does not carry within itself the power to make human life human and to transform creation. Humanity should again turn towards the cross that stands both as a challenge and a hope.

Following the way of the crucified one means having a new self-understanding, an a new vision of the future. Following the way of the cross is to reject the ultimate validity of any status quo or ideology, and to struggle for justice and human dignity. The future towards which humanity moves is God's future. It is the future of a renewed and reconciled humanity in a transformed and sanctified creation.

Some ecumenical considerations

I want to conclude this paper with the following observations:

1. The central thesis of my brief presentation was that human

beings are a theological reality and as such they have to be dealt with in a theological perspective. Anthropology has always been from the early period of church history an important chapter of Christian theology. It seems to me that anthropology has considerably lost its centrality, particularly in Western theology. I do not want to spell out the root causes now. I would like to emphasize that the anthropological dimension is crucial for Christian theology, otherwise the latter is reduced merely to metaphysics. Orthodox theology may play a major role in helping Western theology recover its theo-anthropology. Significantly enough, the World Council of Churches has concluded just a year ago a study-process on *Humanum*. In considering the vital importance of anthropology for ecumenical thought and action, the Uppsala (1968) assembly had decided to set within the programmatic structure of the WCC a special programme on *Humanum* Studies. This helped to clarify and sharpen various aspects and dimensions of the relation of theological issues to human self-understanding and existence. This issue must remain a permanent concern and a priority for the ecumenical movement as it attempts to consider God, humanity and creation in a holistic perspective.

2. Creation is another important subject which has been moved to the periphery of our theological thinking. Creation is not only the context in which human life is perpetuated; it is also the place where the relationship between humanity and God takes place. Creation ought to acquire a dominant place in our theology as was the case with Patristic theology. It is important to note that the WCC through some of its programme units, such as Faith and Order, Church and Society and *Humanum* Studies, and some of the assemblies has, in one way or another, taken up this issue. However, Christocentricism still prevails in the ecumenical movement. This needs to be corrected.

3. A third issue which, in my view, requires serious attention is the inseparable relationship that exists between humanity and creation. This has a biblical basis. It must be given due consideration in our theological thinking and education. Theology does not deal with God, humanity and creation in isolation from one another, but always in their dynamic interrelatedness. More and more human problems are finding an echo in theology. Ecological questions that are increasingly acquiring focal attention in present societies must somehow be addressed by theology. In fact, biblically-based Chris-

tian theology, more than any human discipline, has the obligation to deal with ecological issues that have immediate repercussions for the self-understanding of human beings, their relationship with God, and their role in creation.

Notes

1. The text has appeared in Maurice Assad, editor, *Tradition and Renewal in Orthodox Education*, WCC, 1976, pages 71–80.

4

The Holy Spirit in Orthodox Pneumatology

A paper read to the Orthodox consultation on the theme of the Canberra assembly held in Crete, Greece, 25 November–4 December 1989.[1]

This paper is not a treatise on *de spiritu sancto*. It aims at identifying some of the peculiar features of Orthodox pneumatology[2] which may offer new perspectives and challenges to the ongoing ecumenical assessment of the theme of the Canberra assembly: 'Come, Holy Spirit—Renew the Whole Creation'.

It is important to spell out two basic teachings of Orthodox theology.

First, God is not an abstract divinity. God is a revealed reality. While remaining absolutely transcendent and incomprehensible, God has revealed himself in time and space.[3] The revealed God cannot be conceived outside the three persons. Therefore, the Trinity is not a speculative theory or a kind of metaphysics. It is the fundamental reality of Christian faith. The whole of Christian life in all its dimensions and manifestations is the reflection of the grace of the Holy Trinity.

Secondly, not only is God a Trinity, but God also acts as a Trinity. The persons of the Trinity may act differently but not independently. The act of one person is the act of the whole Trinity. The Orthodox Church emphasizes the wholeness, the plenitude as well as the cosmic dimension of God's creative and redemptive acts and understands the economy of the Holy Spirit in a Trinitarian perspective, rejecting the 'Christomonism' of the West.

The Holy Spirit and the Trinity

The person of the Holy Spirit remains mysterious. The biblical titles and images are abundantly used by the Eastern Fathers. He is the

Spirit of God, the Spirit of Christ, the mind of Christ, the Spirit of the Lord, the Spirit of adoption, of truth, of liberty, of wisdom, of understanding, of humility, of counsel, of might, of knowledge, and so on.[4] The following images are also recurrent in the writings of the Fathers and particularly in Orthodox liturgy: 'living fire', 'source of life', 'distributor of grace', 'comforter of those in pain', 'tree of life', 'revealer of mysteries', 'vessel of teaching', 'gate of repentance', 'terrible wind', 'source of good', 'life-giving stream', 'true light', 'wine of wisdom', 'giver of mercy', 'cup of immortality', 'life-giving breath', and so on.[5] The Holy Spirit is the maker of 'all things', yet incapable of being comprehended by the creature.[6] The Spirit is 'God's gift'[7] and 'its proper and peculiar title is Holy Spirit'.[8]

It is important to note that the names given to the Holy Spirit denote a divine subject. They also describe a divine energy. Despite the mystery that surrounds the Holy Spirit, Orthodox pneumatology affirms that he is a person, but the least manifested, the least known of the three persons of God. It is rather the grace of the Holy Spirit that is active in the human creature and creation. The Holy Spirit has no definite name or static form of his own. He reveals himself under different names, in different ways and forms. He 'blows where it wills'. We 'hear the sound of it' (John 3:8). We see his 'signs'. But his divine person remains always hidden, not revealed.[9]

God is a unity of three hypostases[10] who are not self-existent beings, but always in mutual relationship. A major concern of Orthodox theology has been to affirm the distinctiveness of each hypostasis and at the same time to maintain the uniqueness of the Father as the sole principle (monarchy), the source and cause of Godhead. Thus, the Son is generated by and the Holy Spirit proceeds from the Father. In other words, they do not derive their existence from a common *ousia*, but from the hypostasis of the Father who draws his being from himself.

The specificity of each hypostasis stems from his relationship to the common source—the 'divine source' of the Father. The Holy Spirit receives his existence from the Father and his mission from the Son.[11] The inter-Trinitarian unity is so intimate that, as Symeon the New Theologian says, we cannot even speak in terms of first, second and third hypostases.[12] God is 'undivided in separate persons'[13] without confusion of hypostases, division of *ousia*, or subordination. The Holy Spirit is counted third only in the order of transmission. He is co-substantial and co-equal with the Father and the Son.[14] All divine attributes are also the attributes of the Spirit.[15]

40

Orthodox theology always puts a kind of functional priority (monarchical Trinity) within the Trinity: from the Father through the Son and in the Holy Spirit.[16] But it is in the power of the Holy Spirit that we recognize the Father in the image of the Son (eucharistic Trinity): 'When we receive gifts, the first that occurs to us is the distributor, next we think of the sender, and then we lift our thoughts to the fountain and cause of the boons.'[17] Therefore, the Triune God becomes accessible to human beings by the Holy Spirit.

The Holy Spirit does not reveal his person, as the Son does in Jesus. He only communicates his uncreated grace to men and women. The person of the Holy Spirit is only revealed through his gifts.

The Holy Spirit: co-creator with the Father and the Son

The Holy Spirit is not only co-substantial and co-eternal but also co-creator with[18] the Father and the Son.[19] He 'does all things that God does'. He is 'the finger of God' manifesting God's creator-spirit.[20] An Armenian hymn says: 'The Holy Spirit was, is and always will be; he has neither a beginning nor an end; but always with the Father and the Son, creator and planner.'[21] The cosmos is created out of nothing (ex nihilo); Orthodox theology would say from non-being (ek tou me outos). Creation is the work of the free will of God. It is neither co-eternal with God nor of the essence of God nor a response to any necessity of divine being. It is a created essence. The only motive of God's creation of the cosmos is love. It is an act of love.

Creation is a Trinitarian process: from the Father through the Son in the Holy Spirit. The Father is the 'original cause', the Son the 'creative cause' and the Holy Spirit the 'perfecting cause'.[22] Therefore, the Triune God is the creator of 'all things'. The three persons create together, but each in a special way of his own. The Father is the 'creator of heaven and earth', the Son is the one 'through whom all things were made'. The Holy Spirit is the 'creator of life' (Nicene Creed).

In fact, the Holy Spirit is the 'cause of life',[23] the 'giver of life'[24], the 'breath of life' (Genesis 2:7). It is the 'Spirit of God' that gives life to the creation (Genesis 1:1–27) by being present everywhere in heaven and on earth, filling up all things with life. Symeon describes this in a poetic way: 'You are the cup from which the surge of life streams to me.'[25] Gregory Nazianzus states: 'He breathes where he wills. He is the source of light and life ... He deifies me; he perfects me.'[26] The 'breath of life' is identified by the Eastern Fathers with the Holy Spirit who caused the first man to be made in the image of God (imago Dei).

Not only did God create human beings to be rational creatures with a special responsibility, but he also made them his children. Human beings are the children of God not by nature but by adoption through the Holy Spirit.[27] Thus they stand at the heart of creation. They participate in both the 'spiritual' and 'material' realms of creation. They are an image of the whole creation (imago mundi). They have the God-given task to reconcile the 'spiritual' and 'material' realms.

Creation is a continuous event in the sense that God constantly protects, sustains and perfects his creation through the Holy Spirit. In this Trinitarian creative act the specific function of the Holy Spirit is one of 'completing', 'perfecting', 'guiding', 'governing', 'freeing', 'renewing' and 'fulfilling'.[28] The Orthodox theology of creation (ktisiologia) maintains that the principle of creation is the Father who creates through the Son and perfects his creation in the Spirit. The creation is 'a movement of will', 'an impulse of design' and 'a transmission of power' 'beginning from the Father, advancing through the Son, and completed in the Holy Spirit'.[29] By the Holy Spirit 'all things' are led towards 'their natural and proper end'.[30] It must be noted that this 'perfecting' or 'completing' role attributed to the Holy Spirit does not mean that the Father and the Son are imperfect. They simply want to make things perfect through the Holy Spirit.[31] In fact, the Holy Spirit does not do anything on his own. He implements and brings to completion the work of the Father and the Son.

The role of the Holy Spirit does not include only the last phase of creation. The Spirit is actively and fully involved from the very beginning in all stages and aspects of creation. The creation is full of his energies: 'Creation possesses no gift which does not come to it from the Spirit,' says Basil.[32] The Holy Spirit continues to 'perfect' and 'fulfil' the destiny of creation which is expecting its final liberation and unity in the parousia.

The Holy Spirit: the 'icon' of the Son

As in the creation, in God's redemptive work too the Son and the Holy Spirit are inseparable. Rooted in the Father as the 'primordial cause', the action of the Trinity is a 'double economy' of the Son and the Holy Spirit—the Son revealing the intention of the Father and the Holy Spirit accomplishing it.

The Orthodox understand Christology pneumatologically. The economy of Christ cannot be understood apart from that of the Holy Spirit. *Pascha* (Passover, Easter) and Pentecost are interconnected. The Son and the Holy Spirit have one economy with distinct roles. Irenaeus calls them the 'two hands of the Father'.[33] The economy of the Holy Spirit is neither subordinate nor parallel to the economy of the *Logos*; it is 'its sequel, its continuation'.[34] The role of the Holy Spirit is always 'kenotic', directed to the other. He reveals not himself but the Son. He prepares us to receive Christ. Through him we communicate with the Son and the Son communicates with us, entering into time and space. In different ways and in different forms, but always mysteriously, the Holy Spirit is ever present with the Son in his work: 'Christ is born; the Spirit is his forerunner. He is baptized; the Spirit bears witness. He is tempted; the Spirit leads him up. He works miracles; the Spirit accompanies him. He ascends; the Spirit takes his place.'[35] Hence, the Holy Spirit actualizes and establishes the reality of the presence of Christ as the incarnate word of God.

It is in the presence of the Holy Spirit that Jesus lives, acts, speaks and heals. It is in the Holy Spirit that Jesus is turned towards the Father as well as towards the world, giving his life for the salvation of the world. It is by the Holy Spirit that we are 'Christified' and made the adopted children of the Father.

The Holy Spirit is also the gift of the Trinity. Not only does he reveal to us the knowledge of the Trinity, the vision of the divine light, the mystery of Christ and the kingdom of God, but he also leads us to the Son and through the Son to the Father. The Holy Spirit is the bond between the Father and the Son. He glorifies Jesus the Son and through him God the Father. He glorifies Christ in the creation, manifesting him and uniting us and the creation with him. He also glorifies the creation in Christ to the glory of the Father. Thus, the Holy Spirit gathers together and unites humanity and the whole creation with God and in God.

The glorification of God is only 'completed' when the creation is renewed, redeemed and perfected. God is glorified through the healing and liberation of the creation. The Holy Spirit is both glorifying and unifying God. The mystery of the Holy Spirit is revealed in a Trinitarian perspective of salvation: 'The Son is the image of the Father, and the Holy Spirit is the image of the Son. The one who sees the Son sees the Father and the one who perceives the Holy Spirit perceives the Son.'[36] The Father reveals himself through the Son in the Holy Spirit. And in the power of the Holy Spirit we recognize the Father in the image of the Son. The Holy Spirit is inseparable from the Son, both preceding from him and completing his action. Christ sends us the Holy Spirit and is revealed by the Spirit.[37] Our union with Christ is achieved in the Holy Spirit.

The Holy Spirit: the sanctifier of the creation

It has been pointed out that the specific role of the Holy Spirit is to reveal the glory of the Father and the Son by 'perfecting' the work of the Trinity in creation and redemption. Significantly enough, 'perfecting' is identified by Basil with 'sanctification'.[38] The Father ordains, the Son accomplishes, the Spirit sanctifies. This is a common affirmation of the Orthodox Fathers. In spite of its corrupted state creation is full of the energies of the Holy Spirit and in the process of sanctification. Humanity and creation are perfected when they are in full communion with God and 'filled' with the Holy Spirit.[39] That is why the invocation of the Holy Spirit (*epiklesis*) is central to Orthodox liturgy.

Through the descent of the Holy Spirit the original relationship between God, humanity and creation is re-established; humanity and creation are sanctified: 'The Spirit's descent on him in Jordan was a descent upon us, because of his bearing our body. And it did not take place for promotion to the Word, but again for our sanctification.'[40] The Holy Spirit constantly preserves the creation from falling apart. He vivifies, sustains and sanctifies it in spite of the fall. He is 'the fountain of grace';[41] all the gifts of the creation have their source in the Holy Spirit.[42] He distributes his gifts of grace to all. Those who receive them are saved from 'the dominance of Satan and become the sons of light and inheritors of the kingdom'.[43]

Sanctification is not only a functional attribute of the Holy Spirit; he himself is holy by his very nature.[44] He is the sanctifier 'to whom turn all things needing sanctification'.[45] The whole creation gets its sanctification from the Holy Spirit both in its original and second creation. To put it simply, 'there is no sanctification without the Spirit'.[46] In Orthodox pneumatology sanctification is not only a personal reality; it embraces the whole cosmos. Secondly, it is not an event but a process. The Holy Spirit is constantly being sent as the gift of the Father.[47]

Sanctification has a rich meaning and broad implications in Orthodox theology. It means:

PURIFICATION

Sanctification begins with the purification of the soul which is full of corruption. The greatest sin of humanity is original sin. 'Send us the Spirit of grace to dwell in us to heal the wounds of our souls'[48] is a common prayer in Armenian liturgy. 'Holy Spirit, clean us, the corrupted'[49] is again a hymn sung almost daily in the Armenian Church during Lent. The Holy Spirit is also likened to 'a fire that purifies like gold the smoke of our sins and covers us with the light of glory',[50] or to a 'living fire'—'those who drink it were vivified'.[51]

We are purified from our sins through baptism. The Holy Spirit pours his grace upon the child through the water and *myron* (holy oil), cleans the child from the original sin and strengthens the child to resist all the evils of the world. Through baptism we are regenerated and become 'Spirit-bearers' (charismatic-pneumato-phoros). Baptism is a personal Pentecost. In fact, 'through the Holy Spirit comes our restoration to paradise, our ascension into the kingdom of heaven, our return to the adoption of sons, our liberty to call God our Father, our being called children of light, our sharing in eternal glory'.[52]

In Orthodox liturgical tradition the blessing of water has a profound pneumatological significance. The Orthodox Church believes that the Holy Spirit sanctifies the water, and the latter, in its turn, heals the sickness of soul and body. The purifying function of the Holy Spirit extends over the whole created order. Again, we sing in the Armenian church: 'He (the Holy Spirit) judges the world and purifies it from its sins';[53] also we pray: 'Purify this water with thy grace and power, in order that from those who drink it, the diseases of soul and their body be driven out... those fields that receive it may give harvest abundantly.'[54] The blessing of water as the outpouring of the Holy Spirit is the source of life and renewal for the entire creation.

LIBERATION FROM DEATH

The first man was granted by God the control of nature. But by his free will he chose to be controlled by it and lost his freedom. Man became the prisoner of his flesh.[55] Thus instead of revealing divine plans, creation became the domain and instrument of Satan. The 'prince of the world' established his reign of death in creation. The whole cosmos was plunged into the abyss of chaos, suffering and death. But creation is not a self-centred and self-sufficient entity. Not only is it created by God, but its existence is determined by its relationship with God. Creation is a theocentric reality. God is the centre and the end of it. The true purpose of creation is to fulfil the divine purpose. It has no meaning in itself, only in relation to the purpose for which it is created. Hence, creation is 'groaning' (Romans 8:22), and wants its liberation.

Humanity also groans with the creation, waiting for adoption. The Holy Spirit liberates humanity from dependence upon creation, from the powers of darkness and the reign of evil and death. The Spirit helps humanity to overcome the barriers of division and gives it the freedom and possibility to enter into communion with God: 'Holy Spirit, liberate us from evil works... and make us live by your grace.'[56] The Holy Spirit also liberates creation from the dominance of Satan. Creation receives 'the grace of redemption' and becomes a 'fountain of immortality', a 'gift of sanctification'.[57] In fact, to be liberated from death is to be in freedom. Where the Spirit is, there is liberation (2 Corinthians 3:17).

RENEWAL OF CREATION

The Holy Spirit is the source of renewal *par excellence*. From the very beginning, and continuously, the Spirit renews the whole creation. The incarnation of the Son is the new creation. Christ is the head of the new creation and new humanity. However, the place and role of the Holy Spirit is not secondary in this event of 'new creation'. The Spirit is the Lord of all creation. The event of new creation becomes a living and present reality through the Holy Spirit. In the power of the Holy Spirit the 'new creation' enters into creation and puts it in a dynamic process of renewal. Humanity and creation re-establish their original relation with God.

The Holy Spirit as a source of renewal is one of the favourite themes of Orthodox liturgy. Here are two references taken from the Armenian liturgy: 'The Renewer... who with his grace renews the cosmos... and us from the sins of Adam.'[58] 'Today the heavenly were in joy because of the renewal of the earthly, because of the renewal of creatures; the Holy Spirit descended to the holy upper-room and by him the apostles were renewed.'[59] In fact, the renewal of the whole of humankind as well as heaven and earth, anticipated in the eucharistic *epiklesis*, is the eschatological goal of the whole creation.

DEIFICATION OF CREATION

The ultimate destiny of humanity and creation is deification (*theosis*). The human being is the representative of the cosmos, a 'microcosm'. Men and women are superior to the cosmos. The latter receives the grace through them who are called by God to a supreme vocation: deification, to become by grace that which God is by his nature.

Grace is the transforming and deifying presence of God revealed and poured out by the Holy Spirit. The Spirit transforms us and makes us God-like. Deification is liberation from death. It is re-creation, 'being in Christ', communion with the Triune God. We are not fully human unless we are in communion with God. The Holy Spirit leads humanity to Christ and through him to the Father. Humanity is called also to transform the whole creation in the power of the Holy Spirit. The deification of the cosmos is the restoration of the original order.

The church: 'The permanent *epiklesis* of the Holy Spirit'

The act of *epiklesis* is so important in the life of the Orthodox Church that Nikos Nissiotis rightly describes the church as 'the permanent epiklesis of the Holy Spirit'.[60] The church is a new community created by the Spirit in Christ. It is not a mere institution but a new creation, the image of new humanity.

The coming of the Spirit at Pentecost is the inauguration of a new humanity. Christ and the Holy Spirit together constitute the church's being. The Christ-event and Pentecost[61] should not be confused or separated. They belong to each other. They are two distinct but interrelated actions of God's love. The coming of the Paraclete is the climax of salvation history. Pentecost is the *telos*, the end of revelation in Christ. It is at the same time the *arche*, the beginning of the new creation. The Holy Spirit is the very life of the body of Christ. He transforms the community of sinners into a 'community of saints', into a *koinonia* in God and with God. In fact, the church is the fellowship of the Holy Spirit, the 'covenant... in the Spirit' (2 Corinthians 3:6), the instrument of renewal and liberation, and of the unity of humanity and the whole creation. It is by the Holy Spirit that the church is being sent to the world to accomplish God's purpose in human history and in creation. It is through the Holy Spirit that the church maintains its authenticity, continuity, infallibility and catholicity. The Holy Spirit constantly builds up the church, sustains and strengthens its life. The Holy Spirit safeguards the church's essential unity even in its brokenness and leads it into 'all the truth' (John 16:13).

Irenaeus rightly affirms that 'where the church is, there the Spirit is, where the Spirit is, there also is the church'.[62] All the ministries (*charismata*) of the church are gifts of the Holy Spirit. Each member of the church has his or her own gifts. But not all have the same gifts. The gifts of the Holy Spirit are gifts of *diakonia* (1 Corinthians 12:5) for the enrichment of the church's life and witness. Within these diversities of gifts, a certain hierarchy of charisma is recognized as indispensable for the life and mission of the church (1 Corinthians 12:28).

The sacraments of the church are the manifestations of Pentecost. Through them the gifts of the Holy Spirit are imparted to the faithful. The eucharist is the highest act of 'the permanent *epiklesis*', the church. It is the continuation of Pentecost. The Holy Spirit makes Christ truly present in the eucharist and gives us fellowship with him in bread and wine. As the power of the kingdom the Spirit gives us the foretaste of the new creation. In the eucharist the whole creation is transfigured. The *epiklesis* is the supreme moment in Orthodox liturgy; it is central to the sacramental action of the church. In fact, 'Come, Holy Spirit, and dwell in us, purify, renew and sanctify us' is a common and almost daily prayer in Orthodox life. The church becomes a sacramental reality in history through the invocation of the Holy Spirit.

Epiklesis displays four important dimensions:

1. It is the precondition and also a spiritual preparation for the outpouring of the Holy Spirit promised by Christ to the church. The Holy Spirit is the grace of God acting in the church. He fills the church with life, renews and revitalizes its life.

2. Through *epiklesis* not only is the church renewed but it is also

sent to the world for the world's renewal in justice and freedom. All humanity and the whole of creation are dynamically interrelated in this renewal process in the power of the Holy Spirit.

3. The institutional church is only a means, a channel of charismatic life. Therefore, it is itself exposed to the judgment of the Holy Spirit. *Epiklesis* challenges the self-sufficiency of the church and makes it totally dependent on the grace of God. It reminds the church that it is not only a historical reality but also an eschatological event. It is the *eschaton* that determines the church's very being, its *raison d'être*.

4. *Epiklesis* prepares the church for the second coming of Christ. The descent of the Holy Spirit is the anticipation of the ultimate fulfilment. It is the beginning of cosmic transfiguration. It is the coming of the *eschaton*. In fact, the Holy Spirit brings eschatology to history.

The Holy Spirit and the ecumenical movement

One of the significant achievements of the ecumenical movement, undoubtedly, is the rediscovery of the pneumatological dimension as vital for the life and witness of the church. The ecumenical movement itself is the work of the Holy Spirit. The emergence of pneumatology in 'ecumenical theology'—though still incomplete and insufficient—was a reaction against the growing Christocentricism, theological rationalism and ecclesiastical institutionalism of the West. It was also due to the growing participation of the Orthodox churches in the ecumenical fellowship and their insistence on a Trinitarian theology.[63] A Holy Spirit-centred theme proposed for the Canberra assembly may have concrete implications for the future of the ecumenical movement at least in a threefold sense:

◇ First, it may considerably reduce the excessive Christocentricism of the WCC and sharpen the crucial importance of a Trinitarian pneumatology for fthe ecumenical movement.

◇ Secondly, it may breathe a new vitality, creativity and dynamism into the ecumenical movement which has started to lose much of its 'spirituality' and 'charisma'.

◇ Thirdly, it may provide new perspectives for dealing with the issues and concerns presently on the agenda of the WCC, such as the question of spirituality, the concern for the wholeness and integrity of God's creation, the search for a *marturia*-centred *diakonia* (service based on self-sacrificial witness), the imperative of sharing resources, the search for Christian unity, the renewed attention given to congregational life, the growing commitment for justice and peace, and dialogue with other faiths. These and all other issues that are being grappled with by the WCC may be challenged and enriched by a Trinitarian pneumatology.

Notes

1. It is published in Gennadios Limouris, editor, *Come, Holy Spirit—Renew the whole creation*, Holy Cross Orthodox Press, 1990, pages 61–81. It has also appeared in *The Ecumenical Review*, volume 42, Numbers 3–4, July-October 1990, pages 197–206 with the title: 'The Assembly Theme: More Orthodox Perspectives'.

2. Unlike Christology, pneumatology has not undergone a systematic and lengthy treatment in Orthodox patristic theology. Basil can be rightly considered an authority in Orthodox pneumatology. The contribution of Athanasius, Gregory of Nyssa and Gregory of Nazianzus to the development of pneumatological thinking cannot be underestimated. Rich materials can be found particularly in Orthodox hymnology, sacramental theology and spiritual literature.

3. Orthodox theology makes a clear distinction between the incomprehensible essence of God (*ousia*) and the energies (*energia*) of God. The latter are also incomprehensible, but they can be communicated to people through the Holy Spirit.

4. Compare: 1 Corinthians 2:11; Romans 8:9–15; 2 Corinthians 3:17; Galatians 4:6; John 14:17; 15:26; 16:13.

5. *Book of Sacraments* (in Armenian), Jerusalem, 1807, pages 113, 323; *Armenian Church Hymns* (in Armenian), Antelias, 1980, pages 30, 82, 114.

6. Gregory of Nazianzus, 'The Theological Orations', in Edward R. Hardy, editor, *Christology of the Later Fathers*, SCM Press, 1972, page 201.

7. Athanasius, 'Tome or Synodical Letter to the People of Antioch', in P. Schaff and H. Wace, editors, *A Select Library of Nicene and Post Nicene Fathers of the Christian Church*, volume IV, Eerdmans, 1957, page 357.

8. Basil, 'On the Spirit', in P. Schaff and H. Wace, editors, *A Select Library of Nicene and Post-Nicene Fathers of the Christian Church*, volume VIII, Eerdmans, page 15.

9. It is mainly for this reason that in Orthodox liturgy prayers are usually

addressed to the Father, to the Son or to the Trinity. Prayers addressed directly to the Holy Spirit are very rare.

10. God is one essence (*ousia*) in three persons (hypostases). This formulation of Cappadocian Fathers has become the criterion of Orthodox Trinitarian theology. Originally the terms *ousia* and hypostasis were used synonymously to refer to 'being' or 'nature'. This confusion was complicated further by the fact that the Latin equivalent for the Greek *hupostasis* was *substantia*. The Cappadocians made a sharp distinction between hypostasis and *ousia*. For them *ousia* (substance) refers to the nature of Godhead, to that essential being which Father, Son and Spirit have in common. Hypostasis (*persona*) refers to the inner distinction of Godhead.

11. The Eastern Fathers have always insisted on the radical difference between the procession of the Holy Spirit from the Father and the manifestation of the Holy Spirit through the Son.

12. 'The Father is not first even though He is the cause of the Son, nor is the Son second even though He comes from the Father, nor is the Holy Spirit third, though He proceeds from the Father' (Basil Krivocheine, *St. Symeon the New Theologian— In the Light of Christ, translated by A.P. Gythiel, New York, St. Vladimir's Seminary Press, 1986, page 259.)*

13. Gregory of Nazianzus, 'The Theological Orations', in Edward R. Hardy, editor, *Christology of the Later Fathers*, SCM Press, 1972, page 202.

14. Gregory of Nyssa, 'On the Holy Spirit', in P. Schaff and H. Wace, editors, *A Select Library of Nicene and Post-Nicene Fathers of the Christian Church*, volume V, Eerdmans, page 320. Basil says that in saying Father, Son and Holy Spirit we do not enumerate them by computation, but assert their individuality, namely the distinctiveness of each hypostasis. Any numerical idea is not applicable to Trinity. It is only imposed upon us by language.

15. Gregory of Nyssa, 'On the Faith', in P. Schaff and H. Wace, editors, *A Select Library of Nicene and Post-Nicene Fathers of the Christian Church*, volume V, Eerdmans, page 330.

16. The monarchy of the Father does not imply subordination of the Son and the Holy Spirit. It is a kind of monarchy that manifests itself only in, by and for the Trinity. This is a basic point in Orthodox Trinitarian theology.

17. Basil, 'On the Spirit' in P. Schaff and H. Wace, editors, *A Select Library of Nicene and Post-Nicene Fathers of the Christian Church*, page 23. Nazianzus has a similar remark: 'From the Spirit comes our new birth, from the new birth our new creation, and from the new creation our deep knowledge of the dignity of Him from whom it is derived' ('The Theological Orations', in Edward R. Hardy, editor, *Christology of the Later Fathers*, SCM Press, 1972, page 211.)

18. Basil makes an important distinction between with and in. In relation to Godhead the Holy Spirit is with the Father and the Son. While in relation to his operation in human beings, he is in them (op. cit. pages 39–40).

19. Gregory of Nyssa, replying to those who exclude the presence of the Holy Spirit in the creation, says sarcastically: 'What was the Holy Spirit doing at the time when

the Father was at work with the Son upon the creation? Was He employed upon some other works ... If, on the other hand, He was present, how was it that He was inactive? Because He could not, or because He would not, work?' ('On the Holy Spirit', in P. Schaff and H. Wace, editors, *A Select Library of Nicene and Post-Nicene Fathers of the Christian Church*, volume V, Eerdmans, page 320).

20. Nazianzus, 'The Theological Orations', in Edward R. Hardy, editor, *Christology of the Later Fathers*, SCM Press, 1972, page 212.

21. *Armenian Church Hymns*, Antelias, 1980, page 270.

22. Basil, 'On the Spirit' in P. Schaff and H. Wace, editors, *A Select Library of Nicene and Post-Nicene Fathers of the Christian Church*, volume VIII, Eerdmans, page 23. It is important to note that Orthodox ktisiology rejects both deism and pantheism and binds together God's transcendence and immanence.

23. *Holy Week* (in Armenian), New Julfa, 1895, page 521. The Holy Spirit as the cause and giver of life is a dominant figure in the liturgy of the Armenian church. Basil in his treatise 'On the Holy Spirit' also makes constant reference to the Holy Spirit as 'supplier of life'.

24. *Liturgical Book* (in Armenian), Antelias, 1986, page 435.

25. Basil Krivocheine, *St. Symeon the New Theologian—In the Light of Christ*, translated by A.P. Gythiel, New York, St Vladimir's Seminary Press, 1986, page 262.

26. Nazianzus, 'The Theological Orations', in Edward R. Hardy, editor, *Christology of the Later Fathers*, SCM Press, 1972, page 214.

27. Athanasius, 'Discourse II', in P. Schaff and H. Wace, editors, *A Select Library of Nicene and Post-Nicene Fathers of the Christian Church*, volume IV, Eerdmans, page 380.

28. Nyssa,
'On the Holy Spirit', page 320; 'On the Faith', page 338. Both in P. Shaff and H. Wace, editors, op. cit.

29. Ibid., page 320.

30. Basil, 'On the Spirit', in P. Schaff and H. Wace, editors, op. cit., page 15.

31. Ibid., page 24.

32. Ibid.

33. Irenaeus, 'Against Heresies', in A. Roberts and J. Donaldson, editors, *The Ante-Nicene Fathers*, volume I, Eerdmans, 1957, page 369.

34. Vladmir Lossky, *Orthodox Theology: an Introduction*. translated by Ian and Ihita Kesarcodiwatson, New York, St Vladimir's Seminary Press, 1978, page 156.

35. Nazianzus, 'The Theological Orations', in Edward R. Hardy, editor, *Christology of the Later Fathers*, SCM Press, 1972, page 211.

36. Basil Krivocheine, *St. Symeon the New Theologian—In the Light of Christ*, translated by A.P. Gythiel, New York, St Vladimir's Seminary Press, 1986, page 268.

37. Symeon, speaking about this specific role of the Holy Spirit as the one revealing Christ, also describes the Holy Spirit as 'the mouth of the Lord' (Basil Krivocheine, op. cit. page 267).

38. Basil, 'On the Spirit', in P. Schaff and H. Wace, editors, *A Select Library of Nicene and Post-Nicene Fathers of the Christian Church*, volume IV, Eerdmans, page 34.

39. Ibid., pages 24–26.

40. Athanasius, 'Discourse I', in *A Select Library of Nicene and Post-Nicene Fathers of the Christian Church*, volume IV, Eerdmans, page 333.

41. *Book of Sacraments*, Jerusalem, 1807, pages 109, 193; *Armenian Church Hymns*, Antelias, 1980, pages 49, 51.

42. Basil, 'On the Spirit', in P. Schaff and H. Wace, editors, *A Select Library of Nicene and Post-Nicene Fathers of the Christian Church*, volume IV, Eerdmans, page 35.

43. *Book of Sacraments*, Jerusalem, 1807, page 193.

44. Nazianzus, 'The Theological Orations', in Edward R. Hardy, editor, *Christology of the Later Fathers*, SCM Press, 1972, page 212.

45. Basil, 'On the Spirit', in P. Schaff and H. Wace, editors, *A Select Library of Nicene and Post-Nicene Fathers of the Christian Church*, volume IV, Eerdmans, page 35.

46. Ibid., page 24.

47. Nyssa, 'On the Holy Spirit', in P. Schaff and H. Wace, editors, *A Select Library of Nicene and Post-Nicene Fathers of the Christian Church*, volume V, Eerdmans, page 323.

48. *Liturgical Book*, Antelias, 1986, page 435.

49. *Armenian Church Hymns*, Antelias, 1980, page 175.

50. Ibid., page 455.

51. Ibid., page 323.

52. Basil, 'On the Spirit', in P. Schaff and H. Wace, editors, *A Select Library of Nicene and Post-Nicene Fathers of the Christian Church*, volume IV, Eerdmans, page 323.

53. *Armenian Church Hymns*, Antelias, 1980, page 455.

54. *Book of Sacraments*, Jerusalem, 1807, page 96.

55. Basil Krivocheine, *St. Symeon the New Theologian—In the Light of Christ*, translated by A.P. Gythiel, New York, St Vladimir's Seminary Press, 1986, *page 272*.

56. Khorhertader, *Holy Liturgy* (in Armenian), Jerusalem, 1927, page 11.

57. *Book of Sacraments*, Jerusalem, 1807, pages 67–68.

58. *Armenian Church Hymns*, Antelias, 1980, page 93. See also pages 100, 113, 116.

59. Ibid., page 200.

60. Nikos Nissiotis, 'Called to Unity: the Significance of the Invocation of the Spirit for Church Unity', in *Lausanne 77, Faith and Order* Paper No. 82, WCC, 1977, page 54.

61. Pentecost as the gift of the Holy Spirit displays three important dimensions which need to be constantly kept in mind in our ecumenical fellowship: first, it is a gift to all God's people (Acts 2:4). Secondly, it is a gift of unity (Acts 2:1). Thirdly, it is a gift of diversity (Acts 2:3).

62. Irenaeus, 'Against Heresies', in A. Roberts and J. Donaldson, editors, *The Ante-Nicene Fathers*, volume I, Eerdmans, 1957, page 431.

63. For a brief yet comprehensive outline of the development of pneumatology in the WCC, see Konrad Raiser, 'The Holy Spirit in Modern Ecumenical Thought', in *The Ecumenical Review*, volume 41, number 3, July 1989, pages 375–87.

5

'Come, Holy Spirit, Renew the Whole Creation': Its Implications for the Middle East

A paper presented to the regional pre-assembly meeting held in Cairo, Egypt, 5–7 May 1990.

The assembly of the World Council of Churches in Canberra, Australia has as its main theme: 'Come, Holy Spirit—Renew the Whole Creation.' The sub-themes are: 'Giver of Life—Sustain your Creation!'; 'Spirit of Truth—Set us Free!'; 'Spirit of Unity—Reconcile your People!'; 'Holy Spirit—Transform and Sanctify Us!'. It is significant to note that this was the first time in the history of the WCC that an assembly chose a Holy Spirit-centred theme as the theological context for its deliberations and actions.

On this very point allow me to be personal. I happened to be among the few people who played an active part in selecting, shaping and developing this theme. The process was not an easy one. We were confronted with a number of difficulties. Some feared that a theme on the Holy Spirit might be interpreted as an encouragement to para-church movements both within and outside the institutional churches. Others thought that it would be too ecological. Some went so far as to consider it void of any Christological foundation, and hence of ecclesiological implications. I was one of the staunch advocates of this theme for the following main reasons:

1. Those of us who have participated in the life and work of the WCC will certainly have realized that the theology of the council has always been and is, to a large degree, Christocentric. It is imperative that the Western Christomonism of the WCC is balanced by a pneumatological dimension spelling out more clearly the

interrelatedness of Christology and pneumatology. In fact, I consider this vital for the future of the ecumenical movement.

2. The theme under consideration displays a rich diversity of biblical-theological insights and perspectives. It may, therefore, contribute immensely to the development of biblically-based theological thinking in the churches and in the WCC. This has become a must in view of the growing gap between biblical theology and contemporary theology.

3. It is a fact that not only contemporary theology but also Christian life today suffers from the absence of the Holy Spirit. In other words, that vital dimension of our Christian life and witness which is often referred to as 'spiritual' has become so overwhelmed by mundane concerns that we really need the revivifying presence of the Holy Spirit.

4. A pneumatological theme also has a crucial significance for the following two reasons: first, most of the problems that the churches are facing in their actual life and mission on local, regional and global levels—the question of unity, the struggle for justice and peace, dialogue with other faiths, growing zeal for new evangelism to modern societies, concern for the renewal of the church and for human community—can be meaningfully related to this theme and vice versa. Secondly, the theme also has concrete and immediate relevance to many of the major issues of the present world—the increasing concern about ecological crises, threats emerging from the dominance of science and technology, questions related to justice, peace and human rights, and so on.

5. Last but not least, as an Oriental Orthodox theologian with a rich mystical-spiritual theological heritage, and as a Christian living in the pluralistic society of the Middle East, I firmly believe that the Canberra theme has a special and direct bearing to the life and witness of the churches in this region of the world. Let me attempt to identify, in outline, some of its basic implications.

The Spirit of life

The Holy Spirit is the Spirit of life. The Triune God is the source of life. This is a basic affirmation of our faith. The Holy Spirit is the giver of life; he is the life-giving presence of the Triune God. Like breath, he inspires and empowers life in human beings and in the whole creation. Without the presence of the Spirit all things in the creation 'die and return to their dust' (Psalm 104:29). The Holy Spirit is not only the generator of life, but also the one who sustains it. The images given to the Spirit in the Bible—fire, wind, water, dove, and so on—point to the life-giving and life-sustaining work of the Holy Spirit. It is important to spell out some significant features of life given to human beings and creation:

◇ Life is a gift of God. It is not the possession of either human beings or creation. They are called to preserve and enrich it for the sake of all, and to the glory of God.

◇ Life is sacred; not because the giver of life is holy, but because it is given with a good intention, namely, for the building of the kingdom of God.

◇ Life is given in its wholeness. It embraces physical, biological and spiritual dimensions which are manifested in the created order as an interrelated whole. Any notion of dualism—which, in one way or another, prevailed for a long time in Western theology—is alien to biblical theology. God created life as one whole. The distinctions are within one indivisible whole. The saving work of Christ included the whole of life, namely, sinful humanity and the distorted creation.

The cosmic nature of salvation is strongly emphasized in Orthodox theology. The integrity of creation which has now become a major ecumenical concern is, therefore, a God-given reality, and its preservation a God-given responsibility to humans. We are called to protect and to enrich creation; to be its guardian.

But creation in all its dimensions and manifestations is threatened because human stewardship of creation has been changed into its exploitation. Major advances in science and technology have alienated human beings from the true source of life and have made them the centre of creation, and thus increased the threat to human survival. The ecological survival of the entire planet is at stake. Human life is on the verge of total annihilation.

The repercussions of these global threats are being most acutely and explicitly manifested in the Middle East. The illegal appropriation of lands, the forced change of the identity of nations and geographical localities, the emerging religio-ideological doctrines that strongly question the credibility of progress and development, the politico-economic manipulation of the majority by the ruling classes, the environmental deterioration caused by pollution and erosion, military conflicts, racial hatred, the creation of regional superpowers—to mention only some of the major issues that we are constantly faced with—put the very existence of peoples, groups and nations in a state of extreme jeopardy. Human life is taken for granted in this part of the world. Human values are often considered archaic and obsolete. Ethical standards are often ignored. The gift of God's creation is regarded as the possession of a few people and nations. The Middle East, perhaps more than any region, is directly exposed to disintegration and destruction.

The churches of the region are faced with the following urgent tasks:

◇ First, they have to go back to the original sources of biblical and patristic theology since their theology has changed so much of its identity due to the invasion of the norms and values of modern secular humanism into the Middle East.

◇ Secondly, they need to develop a Trinitarian theology of creation which emphasizes the wholeness, integrity and sacredness of life.

◇ Thirdly, they must rediscover the kind of pneumatology which affirms the right relationship of humanity to creation and human responsibility for the safeguarding of God's gift of life.

The Spirit of renewal

The Holy Spirit is the Spirit of renewal. The renewal of the whole of life and creation is the work of the Holy Spirit in both the Old and New Testaments. He transforms and sanctifies the brokenness of creation which becomes 'a new creation' (2 Corinthians 5:17) through the salvific work of the crucified and risen Christ. Transformation and sanctification of the creation is essentially re-creation, rebirth—simply renewal. The Holy Spirit is the source and the agent of renewal. He not only creates and sustains the creation, but breathes new life into it, leading it from alienation, corruption and death into new life in Christ. Everything in creation is made new through Christ in the power of the Spirit.

Baptism is an act of renewal by which a human being is cleaned from original sin, and incorporated into the 'new creation', the church. Renewal is not, therefore, a human initiative. It is an act of

God through Christ in the power of the Holy Spirit. It is also a process by which, through the guidance of the Spirit, the people of God constantly grow in their faithfulness to the will of God—incarnating the imperatives of the Gospel in their life and in the life of society.

Renewal is not confined to the church. It embraces the whole of humanity, history and creation. The Holy Spirit acts through the church in the world. The church is the 'new creation' brought into existence and constantly being built up and sustained by the Spirit. Its fundamental vocation is to reveal the renewing presence and work of the Spirit in all creation by fighting against the abuse and destruction of the whole of humanity and creation, and becoming a sign and an instrument of renewal and transformation. Renewal doesn't mean ignoring the past and old things, but rather, having a renewed awareness of continuity as well as a critical openness to the world, to history and to the future. It means questioning self-centredness and self-sufficiency, and having the courage to face new realities and challenges. With such an understanding of renewal the churches of the region have always experienced the renewing power of the Holy Spirit throughout their history in spite of vicissitudes, upheavals and persecutions of one sort or another.

It has become now almost commonplace to state that the present age is one of tremendous changes. Radical and impact-making changes are taking place around us every moment. In addition to its own internal changes, the Middle East is appropriating new norms of life, new patterns of thinking, new models of community which are often foreign to our precepts, to our philosophy of life. The wind of renewal that is blowing around us is not always healthy. It is sometimes deadly. Our churches should discern between the signs of genuine renewal that builds up and transforms, and the false renewal that degenerates, disintegrates and destroys. Our churches must make a real distinction between human-centered changes and the renewal that is empowered and guided by the Holy Spirit.

Here are pivotal questions that we must constantly grapple with:

◇ How can our churches deal, in a critical but constructive way, with the so-called 'renewal' movements, new forms of Christian life and new norms of Christian ethics that are, with rapid pace indeed, moving from the periphery of our life into those spheres which used to be considered untouched and untouchable?

◇ How can our churches come out of their ghetto existence and respond to new realities and perspectives for the renewal of their life and witness?

The theme of Canberra is a challenge to our churches for serious self-assessment and self-renewal. It is also a call to continue, more responsibly, their God-given mandate to become the true sign of the renewal of the whole of humanity and creation in a situation of uncertainty and despair.

The Spirit of unity

The Holy Spirit is the Spirit of unity. The church is born of the Holy Spirit. It is a *koinonia* in the Spirit—a community of people drawn and held together by Christ in the power of the Holy Spirit. In fact, through the Spirit, Christ becomes 'Emmanuel', God-with-us. It is the same Spirit who reconciles us to God in Christ and unites us into a fellowship of God's people (1 John 4:13).

The pneumatological dimension is often overlooked in our Christocentric ecclesiology. It must be rediscovered, otherwise our ecclesiology loses its integrity, authenticity and relevance. Pneumatology and ecclesiology go together. This is, in fact, one of the characteristic features of Orthodox theology. It is important to spell out a few significant aspects of the reconciling presence of the Spirit in the life of the church:

◇ The unity given by the Spirit is a gift of God and not a human achievement. The church as a community of faith is sustained by the 'unity of the Spirit' (Ephesians 4:3) and is called to grow in this unity and translate it into mission in the power of the Holy Spirit.

◇ In this 'unity of the Spirit' social, ethnic and gender differences are transcended (Galatians 3:28), and the 'dividing walls' are broken down. The Holy Spirit builds up the *koinonia* which is grounded in the eucharist and manifested through kerygma and *diakonia*.

◇ The 'unity of the Spirit' is a unity made up of a diversity of gifts. It is alien to uniformity. The otherness and uniqueness of people and groups are well preserved and enriched for the sake of oneness. The *koinonia* of the Spirit is, indeed, an inclusive *koinonia* of unbroken unity in diversity.

◇ The unity that God intends in the power of the Spirit is for the whole of humanity and creation. Therefore, the unity of the church is not a self-sufficient reality. It is only a sign for the eschatological realization of the unity of the entire creation.

The church cannot live without the 'unity of the Spirit'. The reconciling power of the Spirit constantly builds up the *koinonia* in the communion of the Triune God, and sustains it *vis-à-vis* the 'principalities' and 'powers' of the world. The 'unity of the Spirit' makes the church a confessing and witnessing community in the midst of conflicts, tensions and divisions.

We so urgently and desperately need the Spirit of unity in a region where the roots of most of the Christian controversies and schisms are found and still, in one way or other, persist. We have always and most acutely expressed our strong commitment towards unity. We have taken some important steps along these lines. The people at the grass roots are tired of hearing nice slogans about unity. They expect something concrete to be changed in their life, in the relationships of the churches. Unless unity is given some kind of visibility and concreteness on local parish level, it will remain a merely theoretical matter unrelated to the actual life of the people.

It is high time, therefore, that we translate into practice, as far as possible, the theological consensus that we have already reached on major doctrinal issues. For example, the mutual recognition of baptism, the agreement on a fixed Easter date, the development of a common curriculum in the area of theological and Christian education, a common translation of the Bible, joint *diakonia*, shared places of worship and many joint initiatives and common action in several spheres of our common life have become an urgent necessity.

The present day Middle East is such that we can no longer afford to live in isolation. I remember Pope Shenouda once said: 'Christian division started in the Middle East; Christian unity must start from the Middle East.' Our churches should take this challenge seriously. We are living in a region of profound divisions. The occupation of territories by military force, the denial of the rights of self-identity and self-determination, the growing gap between the 'haves' and 'have nots', the increasing tensions between 'modernism' and 'conservatism', and many other factors have brought about more divisions with far-reaching repercussions within Middle Eastern society. Christian unity has to be the ferment of the unity of the

61

whole Middle East. We are called to heal the brokenness of its society and to build relationships of mutual trust among nations and religions. This is a major and crucial task facing our churches.

The Spirit of justice

The Holy Spirit is the Spirit of justice. One of the characteristic images given to the Spirit in the Bible is that he is also the Spirit of truth. In the Old Testament God's truth is expressed in terms of God's justice and righteousness (Deuteronomy 32:4). The people of the Old Testament were chosen by God to live and spread his justice in the world. In the New Testament God's truth is identified with Christ (John 14:16–17). The Spirit of truth guides us 'into all the truth' (John 16:13). He makes us to know the Truth, Jesus Christ, to be free from sin and death (John 8:32) by the liberating truth, and participate in the life of the Triune God. The same Spirit of God who empowered and led Jesus Christ in his ministry of liberation also leads his body to liberate humanity and creation from the dominion of evil, injustice and all 'the world rulers of this present darkness' (Ephesians 6:12) that threaten the life and integrity of creation. Therefore, combating forces, systems and ideologies that generate injustice—the ministry of liberation—is the core of the church's mission.

If we look at the history of our churches from this particular perspective, we can only give thanks to God for making his Spirit of justice a living and life-giving reality in the midst of suffering and persecutions that have marked our presence and witness in this part of the world. Our history became a long chain of misery. But this is not the whole story. Our history also became a living testimony of sacrificial commitment for justice. The same Spirit of justice calls us, at this crucial juncture of the history of the Middle East, to rededicate ourselves, with renewed vision, to the people's struggle for justice and peace.

Often the Middle East is described as a region of continuous conflicts and tensions, sometimes resulting in military clashes. But people hardly ever refer to the root causes of these conflicts—the violation of human rights and flagrant injustice. It is a pivotal task for the churches to confront this reality of the Middle East in the power of the Spirit, and fight against politico-economic structures and racial and ideological trends that perpetuate injustice and escalate confrontation.

The Middle East is not an isolated region. It is an integral part of a world which is increasingly becoming interdependent. Undoubtedly, as churches of the Middle East, we have our own agenda, our own priorities and expectations. An assembly provides a living context of dialogue and interaction. It is important that we maintain the specificity of our way of thinking, of our problems and priorities. But, it is also important that we pursue them in relationship with others, and with a holistic vision.

Like the wind, the Spirit blows where he wills (John 3:8). He creates and renews constantly. His presence is the life-giving, healing and liberating presence of the living Christ. The Holy Spirit is with us and in us if we are able to discern the signs of his presence and perceive the fruits of his work in the world. We are called to 'live by the Spirit' and to 'walk by the Spirit' (Galatians 5:25) since he is the source of life, the agent of renewal, the ground of unity and the Spirit of justice. Let us confront—in the power of the Holy Spirit— the power of death with the promise of life, the state of stagnation with the Spirit of renewal, the pain of division with the joy of unity.

I would like to conclude my presentation with the prayer prepared, just recently, by the Middle East Council of Churches— on the occasion of Pentecost—for peace in the Holy Land:

> O Holy Spirit, tongue of fire, descend upon us as you descended upon the disciples gathered in the upper room for prayer. Sanctify us, free us from the bondage of sin and give us your power to speak with one voice.
>
> Rushing wind, sweep over our lands and make your sound gather again devout people from every nation under heaven. Help us manifest together the victory of life over death given through the resurrection. Make us signs of the living hope and witnesses of your peace.
>
> Giver of life, abide in us, transform our former selves into a new life in faithfulness to God's will. Along with all the others with whom we live, with all nations and peoples we would enter a new time, a time of transformation when hatred is replaced by love, violence by dialogue, condemnation by forgiveness, self-centredness by sharing.
>
> Power of unity, help us to move from the Babel of division, due to ethnic or religious boundaries, to the Pentecost of unity in the diversity of our gifts, traditions, and cultures. Make us ministers of reconciliation among all the

children of Abraham.

Spirit of truth, free us from our alienation from you. Liberate us from the powers and principalities which oppress and alienate. Make us instruments of your justice to which we have been called by prophets, apostles and martyrs. Jesus is risen. The splendour of his realm is through your power, O Holy Spirit, available to all. Make us messengers of the good news, apostles of the peace of Jerusalem, the peace of the Holy Land, the peace of the whole world.

The First Vatican Council and the Petrine Office

*This is the revised text of a paper which was
read to the fourth ecumenical consultation
between theologians of the Oriental Orthodox
Churches and the Roman Catholic Church, in
Vienna, Austria, 11–17 September, 1978.
This was organized by Pro Oriente, a Roman
Catholic ecumenical foundation related to the
Archdiocese of Vienna.[1]*

The First Vatican Council by its definition of the dogma of papal
primacy and infallibility proved to be a significant landmark in the
history of the Roman Catholic Church in general, and West-East
ecclesiastical relations in particular. The dogmatic definitions referred to also made a strong impact on the post-Vatican I ecclesiology of the Roman Catholic Church, raising a poignant reaction from
the Orthodox and Protestant churches. After a period of theological
controversies, theologians from both sides have started critically
reflecting on the issue. I believe that this process of serious reconsi-
deration of the Petrine Office and its ecumenical implications should
continue. This is crucial for the future of the ecumenical movement.

In the first part of this paper, an attempt will be made to identify
those significant aspects and major facts of the nineteenth century
which led the Roman Catholic Church to the dogmatic definition of
primacy and infallibility. This will be followed by a critical scrutiny
of the definitions under consideration with special reference to the
problematic definitions involved. I will conclude my paper with a
few observations for future theological and ecumenical reflection.

Historical background

The French Revolution marked the beginning of a new era in the
political, social and religious history of the world. Its effects were

much more immediate in the West. Thus, socialism coupled with nationalism gradually started to triumph over monarchism. Scientific research claimed supremacy over revealed truth, nature over the supernatural, reason over faith. A complete separation of church and state which had been foreshadowed by the Reformation reached its climax early in the nineteenth century. These developments were followed by the decline of the political power of the papacy. In fact, the loss of papal political power, on the one hand, and the alarming spread of naturalism, rationalism and secularism, on the other, threatened the basic tenets of Roman Catholicism.

The reaction of the Roman Catholic Church to this new situation was on two different, yet interrelated levels: first, the decrease of papal power in world politics would be counterbalanced by the increase of papal power in the Church; and, secondly, a conservative triumphalist theology would emerge as a response to the liberal spirit of the century. This new theological movement, which came to be known as neo-scholasticism or ultra-montanism, would assert the authority of the Roman Church under the monarchical leadership of the pope.

The first formal papal reaction to the 'anti-church' movements came from Pope Gregory XVI. In 1832, he published the encyclical *Mirari Vos* condemning the social and political errors of the times. In 1854, Pius IX pronounced as a dogma the Immaculate Conception of Mary. Furthermore, in 1864, he issued the encyclical of *Quanta Cura* and attached to that a document called *Syllabus Complectens Praecipous Nostrae Actatis Errores*. In the first, papal authority was affirmed as embracing the whole life of the *societas perfecta*. The second one, with its authoritarian and uncompromising language was a declaration of total war against modern trends and ideas. Pius IX took another important step in the direction of centralistic papalism. He appointed a number of non-Italian cardinals, thus broadening the geographical basis of that body as a symbol of the universality of the Roman Catholic Church.

In the politico-religious situation of the century, the convocation of a General Council was more than a necessity. The ground had already been prepared for it. On 26 June 1864, Pius IX publicly announced his intention of convoking a General Council. It is beyond the purview of this paper to make a comprehensive treatment of the First Vatican Council. I would like to single out only a few facts and aspects of the council which I consider to be of crucial importance for a full and accurate understanding of the definitions of papal primacy and infallibility.

1. The aim of Vatican I was to build up an impenetrable wall against the growing liberal trends of the century and assert the supreme authority of the pope. Hence, the council had a defensive character right from the beginning. This, of course, had an immediate bearing on its language, proceedings and decisions.

2. Strong opposition was raised against the council, both in the academic and political worlds, even before its convention. The target of the criticism was the question of papal infallibility. However the anti-infallibilists were a small minority in the council, and did not have a significant influence on its decisions.

3. The definition of the jurisdictional primacy of the Pope did not acquire major attention. The focus of discussion was, both inside and outside the council, the question of papal infallibility. There was great difficulty to find a *formulae concordia*. The '*ex cathedra*' formula softened the opposition. But the addition of '*non autem ex consensu ecclesia*' at the last minute to the last part of *Pastor Aeternus* was a victory for the infallibilists.

4. Vatican I in all its aspects and manifestations was well planned beforehand. Papal control over the entire proceedings and the reporting of the commissions was direct. The bishops were subject to strict rules. New propositions and lengthy discussions were forbidden. The unanimity vote on matters of a dogmatic nature was changed into simple majority vote. There is much evidence which clearly indicates that the dogmatic definitions of the council were not discussed *in extenso*. They were not voted upon freely. They were simply imposed by the Roman Curia.

Vatican I was not an event but a process, in the sense that the definitions it formulated were the culmination of a long-standing conflict between the Roman Church and the European States, and the struggle of the papacy for more power in the Church. It opposed the prevailing conciliarist trends with a strong emphasis on papal power, and with a view of the church as an organized universal structure governed by the pope. In sum, Vatican I became, in the words of Hans Küng, 'a Council, not of hope, but of fear, not of internal reform and renewal, but of reaction and encapsulation against the outside world, not of aggiornamento but of polemical self-defensiveness'.[2]

A Critique of *Pastor Aeternus*

The *Constitutio Dogmatica Prima de Ecclesia Christi*, otherwise known as *Pastor Aeternus* is the most important document of Vatican I. By its content and language it is a typical product of nineteenth-century Catholic theology. The document itself is full of deficiencies, ambiguities and vagueness. It includes the key dogmatic definitions of Vatican I on papal primacy and infallibility. I will first spell out the major points of the two definitions, and then make some comments.

PRIMACY

In its *Decretus pro Graecis* (1439) the Council of Florence had already declared that the '*apostolica Sedes*', henceforth identified with the see of the '*pontifex Romanus*', possessed the universal primacy and the '*plena potestas*' of feeding, ruling and governing the universal church. Vatican I defined with unequivocal terms this claim of the Church of Rome. The following points of *Pastor Aeternus*[3] deserve our attention:

◇ Primacy over the universal church was directly (and not through the church) promised and given to Peter, 'the prince of all the Apostles and the visible head of the whole Church militant'.[4]

◇ The primacy of Peter is not a 'primacy of honor only', but a primacy of 'true and proper jurisdiction'.[5]

◇ This jurisdictional primacy of Peter is transferred to his successor, namely the Bishop of Rome. Therefore, 'whoever succeeds to Peter in this See does by the institution of Christ Himself obtain the primacy of Peter over the whole Church'.[6]

◇ The primacy of the Roman Pontiff does not imply only a power of inspection or direction, but 'full and supreme power of jurisdiction over the Universal Church' in matters pertaining to faith, morals, discipline and government of the church.[7]

◇ The Roman Pontiff possesses the 'fullness of supreme power' (*plenitudo potestatis*), and not 'the principal part' (*potiores partes*) thereof. His power is universal, episcopal, ordinary and immediate.[8]

At this juncture, I want to make some comments:

The nature of the Petrine office is questionable

A correct understanding of the Petrine privilege in the New Testament is of crucial importance for any attempt to evaluate the theology of Petrine office as it is outlined in *Pastor Aeternus*. It is certainly beyond the purpose of this paper to make an exegesis of the well-known verses of the New Testament—namely Matthew 16:18–19; 18:18. In fact, we have a rich literature on this subject. Let me, therefore, only emphasize a few points.

It is important to note that the language of *Pastor Aeternus* is in radical contradiction to that of the New Testament. Clearly, expressions such as *'jurisdictio'*, *'tota plenitudo ... supremae potestatis'*, *'totius ecclesiae caput'*, *'pater et doctor omnium christianorum'*, and so on, do not correspond to the theology of the New Testament, where Peter never appears as 'Vicar of Christ'. In what sense is the Petrine office distinct from the apostolic office? What was the nature and scope of Petrine privilege? The Roman Catholic Church maintains that Peter has a 'trans-apostolic privilege'. This means that the apostles are mere legates of Christ and he alone is given the trans-apostolic power of governing the universal church.

But the fact is that in the New Testament we never come across such a line of demarcation between the apostles and Peter, between apostolic and trans-apostolic power. In other words, the alleged jurisdictional superiority of Peter is alien to the New Testament. The apostolate was one; the apostolic charisma was common to all the apostles who shared the same responsibility given by Christ (Matthew 18:18). The apostolic power of Peter was exactly the same as that of the other apostles. The structure of the apostolic church was not monarchical but collegial. In fact, the commonness of apostolic charisma and the collegial character of the apostolic college constituted the basis of the unity of the early church, which was a communion of the local churches.

Peter may be distinguished from the others, as some New Testament theologians maintain, for his chronological pre-eminence in being the first to confess Jesus Christ as Lord and Saviour. But this never makes him above the apostles. Peter was just one of twelve apostles, as the Church of Rome was one of the local churches founded by the apostles.

Is the Bishop of Rome inheritor of the Petrine pre-eminence?

The history of the Apostolic age does not provide concrete facts to justify the claim of Vatican I that the Bishop of Rome is the inheritor of Petrine privilege. Peter enjoyed a certain pre-eminence among the apostles, to which I have referred. But this privilege was not a lasting nor a transmissible power. It was limited to his person and was not a prerogative of his office as founder of the local Church of Rome. By establishing a church in Rome, Peter naturally exercised his personal prerogatives, and the spirit of Petrine privilege remained attached to the local church of Rome. But this never implies a divinely instituted universal jurisdiction for the Bishop of Rome. In the position of the Roman Catholic church I see three problematic elements:

◇ First, the very concept of individual succession carries with it, ecclesiologically speaking, a fundamental contradiction: how can the Bishop of Rome embody, either potentially or actually, two episcopal authorities, namely local and universal? One is led to think that the office of Rome is absorbed in the universal trans-apostolic office. If it is so, then the claim of Vatican I for universal jurisdictional power lacks any ecclesiological foundation.

◇ Secondly, the bishops, individually or collectively, are not successors of individual apostles but the apostolic college as a whole, and they receive their ministerial power directly from Christ. Therefore, the chair of an apostle and apostolic succession, that is the *sedes* (the chair), and the *sedens* (its occupant), must be differentiated. This is very important. For example, the Coptic Patriarchate of Alexandria is the chair of St Mark; but the Patriarch of the Coptic Church is not the successor of St Mark. Again, St Thaddaeus and St Bartholomew are the founders of the Armenian Church; but the head of the Armenian Church does not claim to be the successor of these apostles. This is true of all the churches which are founded by the apostles.

◇ Thirdly, there are Catholic theologians who still firmly maintain that the pope claims universal jurisdiction not only as the successor of Peter, but also as the Vicar of Christ. This further complicates the problem.

Is the Petrine pre-eminence identical with the Roman Catholic Church?

The Petrine pre-eminence does not belong to the essence of the church, and it can never become a structural element of the constitution of the church. The pre-eminence of Peter was of personal and not institutional nature. Peter can never be regarded as the founder of the 'universal church', as Vatican I teaches. Therefore, the pre-eminence of the Bishop of Rome, which is historically, geographically and politically conditioned, does not imply the jurisdictional primacy of the Roman Catholic Church over the other local churches.

It is important to differentiate between the Petrine privilege and the papacy as it has developed in the course of history. It is a fact that the primacy of the Church of Rome developed mainly on the basis of Rome's political position in the empire. To give a theological substantiation or justification to it is an *a posteriori* attempt. History tells us that for the first time the Bishop of Rome in the person of Stephen II claimed the pre-eminence of Peter in the middle of the third century. Again, Matthew 16:18–19 was quoted for the first time in support of the claim to primacy of the Church of Rome at the beginning of the fourth century.

A shift from primacy of honour (*primatus honoris*) **to primacy of jurisdiction** (*primatus jurisdictionis*).
From the early period of church history a certain primacy of honour was conceded to the Bishop of Rome by the East. This was not a fixed tradition; it was rather done occasionally and with some reluctance. In the course of history however, the status of the Bishop of Rome as *primus inter pares* has gradually developed into a claim for a primacy of jurisdiction. This was mainly due to politico-religious rivalries between East and West. Vatican I dogmatized the jurisdictional primacy and centralistic authority of the pope and made the Church of Rome the centre both of authority and unity of the local churches. Shmemann rightly comments: 'The ecclesiological error of Rome lies not in the affirmation of her universal primacy. Rather, the error lies in the identification of this primacy with "supreme power" which transforms Rome into the *principium radix et origio* of the unity of the Church'.[9]

There is no theological justification for the claim of Rome to be the centre around which all the local churches are to gather. The local churches are equal, as are their bishops. The unity of the church is manifested through the full communion of the local churches. Any local church cannot be the locus of unity. Primacy is a necessity in the church. It is, in fact, a sign of unity. But it does not imply jurisdictional power or a structure of authority over the church.[10]

INFALLIBILITY
Chapter four of *Pastor Aeternus* deals with papal infallibility. After

emphasizing the full and absolute primacy of the pope over the universal church, it states that, by divine assistance, when the Roman Pontiff speaks *ex cathedra*—that is, when exercising his office as the pastor and teacher of all Christians to define a doctrine of faith or morals—he 'possesses of that infallibility which the divine Redeemer willed that His church should be endowed'.[11] According to the teaching of Vatican I, this is 'a dogma divinely revealed', and *ipso facto* the definitions of the Bishop of Rome are 'irreformable of themselves, and not from the consent of the Church' (*ex sese, non autem ex consensu ecclesiae, irreformabiles esse*).[12]

It is important to spell out some of the major problems emerging from this dogmatic definition:

Lack of biblical and apostolic basis

The dogma of papal infallibility lacks any biblical foundation. This is a serious problem, indeed. Hitherto theological speculations and logical argumentation have failed to establish a possible link between papal infallibility and the teachings of the New Testament. Neither does the tradition of the early church provide any substantial support to this effect. In its attempt to legitimize its definition of papal infallibility theologically, Vatican I established a close interdependence between primacy and infallibility. It stated that the pope's jurisdictional primacy extends also to his teaching power. He is not only the first pastor but also the first teacher in the church. Such a linkage is not acceptable for the Orthodox, since primacy is a juridical question, while infallibility touches the core of Christian faith—the nature and meaning of truth.

The 'limitations' of papal infallibility are theoretical

Vatican I made a clear reference to the 'limitations' of papal infallibility. Gasser, the rapporteur of the commission on faith, in his turn, made the following remarks: first, the power of the pope is not absolute or arbitrary; it is limited by both natural and divine law. Secondly, God is *solus infallibilis*. The pope's infallibility is limited to his relation to the church—when he speaks *ex cathedra* on matters of faith and morals. Thirdly, the pope can act, not by virtue of any new revelation, but by virtue of divine assistance.[13]

However, the problem remains: if the pope's obligation to consult a bishop is moral, not juridical according to Vatican I—if the pope can act *non autem ex consensu ecclesiae*—furthermore, if there are no juridical safeguards to control his action, then the so-called 'limitations' established by Vatican I remain theoretical if not artificial. By relating the question of infallibility to the concept of Vicar of Christ, in my judgment, Vatican I went to the other extreme and affirmed the ontological and personal infallibility of the pope.

How can the head act without the consent of the other members of the body?

Vatican I stated in explicit terms that the consent of the church was not a *sine quo non* condition for the exercise of papal magisterial authority. In my view, this is the most vulnerable aspect of the definition. It means that the pope possesses infallibility without the church since he can act without the consent of the church; simply, the pope is infallible *ex sesse*, not *ex consensu ecclesiae*.

The question that Küng raises on this point is a valid one: if the pope can act without the *consensu ecclesiae*, can he also act against the *consensu ecclesiae*? Clearly, Vatican I put the pope above the council. The fact is that the lack of a process of juridical reception of papal *ex cathedra* pronouncements by the whole church, not only made the General Councils of the Roman Catholic Church useless and *consensu ecclesiae* unimportant, but made the papacy a supra-ecclesial structure.

Double subjects of infallibility?

Pastor Aeternus is not clear about the subject of infallibility. According-ing to the elucidations given by Gasser there is only one infallibility, but double subjects of infallibility: the pope (active subject) and the college of bishops united to its head (passive subject). The latter is not an independent entity in itself, and, as such, it cannot oppose the pope. According to the teachings of Vatican I, the infallibility of the pope is identical with that of the church.[14]

One may rightly ask: does the Holy Spirit guard and guarantee the infallibility of the pope and of the church separately? If so, it simply means that the pope is isolated from the church and is in direct relationship with the Holy Spirit. This is heresy. If not, the infallibility of the pope must then be derived from that of the church, and is subject to it.[15]

The position of the Orthodox Churches on this issue can be summarized in the following way: the church as a whole, as a *pleroma* (fullness) is infallible. The council serves as the mouthpiece of the church. Therefore, it is not above the church; it is not infallible in itself. The infallibility of the council is derived from the church and is dependent on it. Hence, the Orthodox reject the dogma of papal infallibility as void of any biblical basis and theological foundation.

EPISCOPATE

Papal primacy and infallibility have a decisive bearing on the jurisdictional status and role of the episcopate in the Roman Catholic Church. According to *Pastor Aeternus* the power that the pope holds is *universalis, episcopalis, ordinaria et immediata*.[16] 'Universal' means that papal power extends over the whole church. 'Episcopal' refers to the threefold power of teaching, ruling and ministering over the entire church as each bishop has it in his own diocese. 'Ordinary' signifies that papal authority is not a delegated one; it is an essential part of his office. 'Immediate' implies that the pope can exercise his power directly on all the faithful without having to pass through the bishop.

It is important to note that Vatican I left the relation of primatial and episcopal power somewhat vague. Obviously, in its endeavour to strengthen the jurisdictional authority of the pope, Vatican I lessened the power of the bishop, though it claims to have 'asserted, strengthened and protected' it 'by the supreme and universal pastor'.[17] In fact, the episcopal power is in its plenitude in the pope, while it is limited in the bishop. The bishops succeed the apostles not by reason of the universal apostolate, but by reason of the episcopate and in their quality as bishops of particular churches. Whatever bishops do, they do in subordination to the pope.[18]

The only limitation on papal power in relation to the episcopate is that the pope cannot abolish it because it is of divine right. The co-existence of primacy and episcopacy in such a pattern of domination and subjugation raises enormous ecclesiological problems. If the episcopal power is of divine right (*lex divini*), and does not come via the pope, then the immediate and ordinary primatial jurisdictional power of the pope violates the power of episcopacy. There exists either duality of power, since both papacy and episcopate are of divine right according to Vatican I, or monarchical power. If the pope and the bishops have the same power, what kind of relation exists between the two subjects of the same power? Are they exclusive or inclusive? How can one reconcile the divine right of the pope with that of the episcopate? Vatican I did not address itself to these critical questions.

Karl Rahner conceives the importance of primacy within the framework of the church's endeavour towards unity and catholicity, and that of the episcopate in the context of the church's existence on the local level.[19] This interpretation does not solve the problem either. Vatican I gave to the pope a supra-episcopal power.

The pope was no longer the first among equals. The papacy became a power structure above the episcopate with full, independent and universal jurisdictional authority. This was definitely based on the theology of the Petrine office. The pope as the Bishop of Rome was almost forgotten in Vatican I.

A few considerations

Hans Küng in his well-known book *Structures of the Church*, speaking about the problematic issues of Roman Catholic ecclesiology, says: 'All difficulties of a theological-dogmatic and practical-existential character that stand in the way of the reunion of separated Christians, and in the way of a general council of the whole of Christendom converge and are rooted in the Petrine office'.[20] I fully agree with this diagnosis. Did the period extending from Vatican I to Vatican II, and especially the post-Vatican II period bring about any real change to the Catholic ecclesiology in general, and to papal primacy and infallibility in particular? Very little, indeed. The substance of the Roman Catholic claims and practices remains the same. The Petrine office stands as a major problem in ecumenical dialogue.

This paper does not seek to be either polemic or irenic. Its intention is to present, in a realistic way, the position of the Oriental Orthodox Churches. It is also a humble attempt to explore the possibilities of a meaningful dialogue between Orthodoxy and Catholicism on these important issues. With this understanding I would like to offer some considerations for a possible re-interpretation of the Petrine office in an ecumenical perspective.

THE NECESSITY OF A NEW THEOLOGY OF PRIMACY

Primacy is practiced in all churches in different ways and on different levels. It has taken different forms and structural expressions in different churches and has been changed within the same church due to historical, geographical and political circumstances. Actually, there are significant differences among our churches about what concerns the nature of the relationship between the head and the episcopal college and in the way the churches understand and exercise primacy.

The Catholic concept of primacy is rooted in the ecclesiology of the Roman Catholic Church, according to which the Universal Church is the sum of local churches. The Petrine office is the centre of this universal, structural and juridical complex. Hence, for the

Roman Catholic Church, primacy is not due to historical contingencies but to divine institution. I have already emphasized that the Roman Catholic attempt to trace back a given model of church organization to the New Testament is valid neither historically nor theologically.

Orthodoxy has always maintained what is called eucharistic ecclesiology, which conceives the structures of the church as a matter of law and right rather than as founded on divine grace. Catholicity is not geographical expansion, organizational uniformity or jurisdictional centralization. It is the church's obedience to the apostolic calling. Therefore, catholicity is essentially of a qualitative nature and is expressed and experienced wherever the eucharist is celebrated with a bishop presiding. There is no geographical and administrative centre for the catholic and universal church. Eucharistic ecclesiology excludes the idea of a supreme power over the local church and the bishop.

The position of a patriarch is regarded in the Orthodox ecclesiology as one of *primus inter pares* among the bishops. A patriarch is not above the episcopal college. He is not *pontifex maximus*, but *episcopus primae sedis*, and does not exercise any jurisdictional power over a diocesan bishop. Hence, neither sacramentally nor theologically is the head distinct from the other members of the episcopal college. He is simply the first in the body.

The concept of primacy on a global scale is foreign to Orthodox ecclesiology. After the great schism in 1054, the Ecumenical Patriarch became *primus inter pares* among the patriarchs of the Eastern Orthodox Churches. The primacy, however, has no jurisdictional or sacramental meaning. Each local church possesses full 'autocephaly'. Among the Oriental Orthodox Churches no church has ever practiced primacy over the entire Oriental Orthodox family. It is time, I believe, that the prevailing Roman Catholic understanding of primacy underwent a significant reassessment. We need a new understanding and a pattern of primacy that will be acceptable to all churches. This will greatly help further the cause of Christian unity.

Let me suggest a few perspectives:

1. The Petrine primacy needs to be reinterpreted in pastoral rather than in juridical terms. It has to be conceived of as a primacy of ministry (*primatus pastoralis*) and service (*primatus servitii*), and not of authority.

2. Primacy is a reality in the church, and not over the church. It is a necessary element for the life of the church. Its role is to safeguard and manifest the unity of the local church as well as the communion of the local churches.

3. Equality of all bishops is the basis of the communion of the local churches. All bishops share the same charisma and ministry. Sacramentally and jurisdictionally there cannot be any power higher than that of the bishop.

4. It is vitally important that jurisdictional primacy, magisterial primacy and primacy of honour be distinguished from each other, and critically examined in view of new jurisdictional, geographical and ecumenical situations and realities.

5. As I see it, there is a growing readiness among the Orthodox (this is, in fact, very apparent in many bilateral dialogues) to ascribe to the Bishop of Rome the *primus inter pares* and *honoris causa* in the communion of local churches. This position of Bishop of Rome, however, will not imply any authority. It will only serve for convening pan-Christian councils and for a symbolic link between the local autocephalous churches. These are, of course, brief hints which need further elaboration and serious discussion.

RETURN TO CONCILIAR AUTHORITY

The Catholic exegists constantly warn us that the fullness of power that the pope holds must not be easily equated with absolutist-monarchical power since the pope is ultimately bound to the church. This may be true *in abstracto* but not *in concreto*. The so-called 'limitations' of papal primacy and infallibility were temporary measures taken by Vatican I aimed to hold a major opposition. The person of the pope remains the supreme locus of infallible authority in the Roman Catholic Church. Vatican I did not allow for any possibility of preventing a pope from making arbitrary decisions, or even acting against the church.

Even Vatican II with its well-known concept of collegiality did not introduce any real change in papal monarchical authority. The exercise of authority is still from above to below. The participation of the whole church in the decision-making process is almost excluded. The worldwide episcopal synod, which was one of the significant achievements of Vatican II, and regular meetings of regional and national conferences of bishops are, indeed, positive developments. But they are all of a consultative nature and their decisions are subject to papal approval.

Both Vatican I and Vatican II completely ignored the conciliar nature of the church and did not leave room for a process of reception by the church. It is vitally important that all future Western developments of ecclesiastical claims of jurisdiction, special privileges and formulations of new dogmas should be discerned on the basis of an ecclesiology which conceives the church as a conciliar communion and the unity of the church as the conciliar communion of the local churches. Therefore, the establishment of conciliar processes and structures is of crucial importance for any major advance in ecumenical dialogue between the Roman Catholic Church and other churches. In my opinion, the emergence of conciliar authority does not minimize the prestige of the papacy, rather it makes the pope the real expressor of *sobornost* (community) as well as the true interpreter of *consensus ecclesia.*

For the Orthodox Churches the unity is the communion of the local churches. Therefore, the papacy with its ecclesiological foundation and implications remains a major obstacle for a real Catholic-Orthodox rapprochement. Dulles has correctly articulated this concern: 'In the course of the centuries, the papacy has become so totally identified with the Roman Catholic tradition that it can hardly serve as a credible organ of ecumenical unity'.[21]

The papacy needs to undergo a process of modification and amplification ecclesiologically as well as administratively speaking. The apologetical approach must be replaced by critical reflection. A processive-evolutionary view should challenge ossified dogmatic teachings. A fresh and critical review of the papacy should constitute one of the priority tasks of contemporary Catholic theology. Vatican I aimed at the centralization of papal power. By doing so it broadened the gulf—already wide and threatening—between the Roman Catholic Church and the non-Catholic churches. Vatican II was a small yet a significant step taken in the opposite direction. The spirit manifested and the direction taken by Vatican II should continue with new impetus and deeper commitment.[22]

Notes

1. The same text with the title of 'The First Vatican Council Reviewed by the Oriental Orthodox Churches—With Special Reference to Primacy and Infallibility' is published in *Wort und Wahrheit*, Revue for Religion and Culture, Supplementary Issue, number 4, Vienna, 1978, pages 124–134.

2. H. Küng, *Infallible? An Enquiry*, translated by E. Mosbacher, London, 1941, page 74.

3. See the text of *Pastor Aeternus* with English translation, H. Edward, *The Vatican Council and its Definitions*, New York, 1871, pages 221–40.

4. Ibid., pages 231–2.

5. Ibid., page 232.

6. Ibid., page 233.

7. Ibid., page 236.

8. Ibid., page 237.

9. A. Shmemann, 'The idea of primacy in Orthodox Ecclesiology' in A. Schmemann, N Afanassieff and N. Kouloumzin, editors, *The Primacy of Peter in the Orthodox Church*, The Faith Press, 1973, page 48.

10. The distinction which J. Ratzinger makes between what he calls 'spiritual-juridical' power and 'administrative' power is very theoretical, and, in my view, does not correspond to the nature and scope of power that Vatican I attributed to the pope. Quoted in K.H. Ohling, *Why do we need the Pope?* translated by R.C. Ware, St Meinrad, 1975, pages 100–101.

11. *The Vatican Council and its Definitions*, New York, 1871, page 240.

12. Ibid.

13. H. Küng, *Infallible*, pages 81–2. See also by Küng, *The Church*, translated by R. Ockendon, Burns and Oates, 1968, pages 449–50.

14. *The Vatican Council and its Definitions*, New York, 1871, page 240.

15. H. Küng, *Structures of the Church*, translated by S. Attanasio, Thomas Nelson & Sons, 1964, page 377.

16. *The Vatican Council and its Definitions*, New York, 1871, page 235.

17. Ibid.

18. K. Rahner and J. Ratzinger, *The Episcopate and the Primacy* New York, 1962, page 18.

19. Ibid., page 28.

20. H. Küng, *Structures of the Church*, translated by S. Attanasio, Thomas Nelson & Sons, 1964, page 224.

21. A. Dulles, 'Papal Authority in Roman Catholicism', in P.T. McCord, editor, *A pope for all Christians?*, New York, 1976, page 65.

22. For primacy and infallibility in the context of 'conciliar fellowship', see also my book *Conciliar Fellowship*, chapter 7.

7

A Critical Assessment
of Four Pro Oriente
Consultations

*A paper prepared for the fifth Pro Oriente
consultation, 18–25 September, 1988,
Vienna, Austria. The main purpose of this
consultation was to review the work of the
earlier consultations, to assess the responses of
the churches and to plan the future course of
events.*

The four Vienna consultations between the theologians of the
Roman Catholic Church and the Oriental Orthodox Churches[1],
organized by Pro Oriente, undoubtedly opened a new and promising chapter in the history of the ecumenical movement in general,
and the theological dialogue between East and West in particular.
Four significant aspects deserve our attention:

1. After fifteen centuries of separation, estrangement and doctrinal
controversies sustained sometimes by mutual anathemata, the very
meeting of church hierarchs and theologians by itself was an event
of great importance. The spirit of critical openness towards each
other, and the sense of belonging to the one and the same church of
God dominated these theological encounters.

2. Although these meetings were not of official nature and scope,
and the participants were not formally mandated by their respective
church authorities, their findings and conclusions found a positive
echo, and created an atmosphere of mutual confidence, comprehen-
sion and *rapprochement* in both the Roman Catholic Church and the
Oriental Orthodox Churches. It is my conviction that the brotherly
meetings of the heads of our churches followed sometimes by
common declarations, the appointment of joint theological commissions on a world level, and the growth of bilateral relations on

regional and local levels during the last fifteen years, were, directly or indirectly, stimulated by the meetings of Pro Oriente.

3. These consultations were exclusively dogmatic in content and highly academic in approach. Serious efforts were made to wrestle with the doctrinal problems of the past in the context of present day situations and vis-à-vis the missiological and pastoral concerns that our churches are faced with. I consider this a vital dimension of any meaningful theological dialogue.

4. Although the Pro Oriente consultations were quite different in their inception, methodology and structure compared with other similar meetings, they have to be evaluated in the broader context of Roman Catholic-Eastern Orthodox encounters of Pro Oriente on the one hand, and Oriental Orthodox-Eastern Orthodox theological dialogue on the other.[2] There exists a considerable degree of similarity between these theological conversations in terms of their agenda, discussion and conclusions.

With these general observations, I will first attempt to identify the major consensus that emerged. Then I will outline my own reaction to the findings of these consultations. I will conclude by spelling out some of the major challenges and prospects pertaining to our future dialogue. In preparation of this paper I have based my arguments and conclusions on the communiqués which summarize the major points of convergence and divergence, rather than on individual papers and ensuing discussions. I must also say that in evaluating the findings of these consultations, I tried to establish a sort of logical order of issues, ignoring totally the chronological sequence of their discussion.

The following major items have been taken up by the Pro Oriente theological dialogue between the Roman Catholic and Oriental Orthodox theologians: local church—universal church; primacy; the ecumenical councils and conciliarity; Chalcedonian christology.

Local church—universal church

The ecclesiology of 'local church'—'universal church' as well as the question of unity have been extensively discussed in relation to the concepts of 'communio' and 'conciliarity'. The following points were regarded fundamental and common in our ecclesiological teachings:

1. The church is one, holy, catholic and apostolic. One and the same church is being manifested both in the 'local church' and in the 'universal church'.[3]

2. The unity of the church is 'Christ's gift to His Church', and not 'merely the result of human endeavours'. The eucharistic communion and the unity of the episcopate are basic factors in the unity of the church—a conciliar communion of the local churches.[4] On this last point no agreement has been reached. For the Roman Catholic Church, Rome was regarded as the centre of this communion. Such a claim was rejected by the Oriental Orthodox side.[5]

Ecclesiology is a crucial area in our theological dialogue. It needs deeper and critical scrutiny. In spite of growing ecumenical openness between our churches, there are still considerable differences in our ecclesiologies. Here are the major ones:

In the first place it is important to remind ourselves that we have different concepts of church.
For the oriental Orthodox the church is *ecclesia localis*.[6] Our ecclesiology does not recognize a so-called 'universal church'. This is not biblical. The church is local always and everywhere. It cannot be otherwise. This is part of church's *esse*. The one, holy, catholic and apostolic church is present in a local church which is *Katholike ekklesia*. Therefore, the local church is not a part of the whole, a subdivision of what is termed the 'universal church'. In Orthodox ecclesiology the church is never considered in terms of its geographical expansion and institutional boundaries. It is essentially the local eucharistic community under the leadership of the bishop. The catholicity of the church is the wholeness, fullness and totality of the body of Christ expressed in the eucharist. A local church represents the whole church in all places and in all times, through communion with other local churches.

Vatican II was, undoubtedly, a turning-point in Roman Catholic ecclesiology. It considerably minimized the universalistic and quantitative elements in the concept of catholicity, and laid the emphasis on the qualitative catholicity, namely, on the local church as being the place where the one, holy, catholic and apostolic church is present.[7] In spite of these new developments the Roman Catholic Church still firmly maintains:

◇ First, 'in and from such individual churches there comes into being the one and only Catholic Church'.[8] This means that the 'universal church' is the sum of the local churches.

◇ Secondly, 'the unique Church of Christ... subsists in the Catholic Church'.[9] Those outside the Roman Catholic Church are not members of the *Una Ecclesia*, though they possess some 'ecclesial reality' and, as such, are in 'imperfect' communion with Rome.[10]

◇ Thirdly, communion with Rome and the Bishop of Rome is a *sine qua non* for the ecclesial authenticity of a local church.[11]

The Roman Catholic Church considers itself a universal fellowship visibly and structurally one throughout the world.
The 'universal church' is made up of local churches which are bound together in union with the Church of Rome, the centre of unity. Although the 'legitimate differences'[12] are given an important place in the communion of the local churches, it is centralism and the legalistic-juridical oneness that make and express the unity of the church. The idea of 'return' is still basic, at least potentially, in Roman Catholic understanding of unity, in spite of considerable ecclesiological modifications introduced by Vatican II as well as the emerging concepts of 'reunion', 're-integration' and 'reconciliation' in contemporary Catholic ecclesiology. For the Roman Catholic Church, any legitimate unity of the church 'is based on a full and substantial communion of local churches among themselves and with the Church of Rome which presides over the whole assembly of charity'. In fact, this position of the Roman Catholic Church is 'beyond compromise'.[13]

The Oriental Orthodox Churches strongly challenge such a concept of unity. I want to spell out four major features of the Oriental Orthodox understanding of unity:

1. The unity of the church is essentially a conciliar life, not in the juridical or canonical sense of the term, but as a real communion in Christ, between the members of the church as well as among the local churches. For the Oriental Orthodox the 'conciliar fellowship' is not only a good and comprehensive 'model' of unity, it also expresses the very nature of unity as a conciliar communion of the local churches. We are firmly attached to such a model of unity because first, it challenges the 'pyramidal vision', and promotes the 'circular vision' of the church in which no church is the centre; and, secondly, it underlines the centrality of the eucharist for the unity of the church.

2. Unity is always a local reality. There can be no structure over the local church. The unity of a local church is maintained and manifested in the eucharist and through communion with other local churches.

3. Unity is both a historical and eschatological reality, a reality 'in space' but also 'in time' linking the past, the present and the future within one tradition and one conciliar fellowship. Unity is not something static, given once and for all. It grows through a dynamic process. Unity is both given and will come. It is a reality both 'behind' and 'ahead' of us.

4. Unity is not a man-made reality, but a gift of God which can only be received and, if lost, rediscovered. Therefore, the unity of the church is neither merger nor theological consensus, but the restoration of eucharistic communion in the apostolic faith.

With such an understanding of unity the Oriental Orthodox Churches believe that the one church has never ceased to exist. The unity of the church has been only obscured due to historical circumstances. The Oriental Orthodox Churches understand themselves as faithfully continuing the apostolic tradition of the one undivided church. They believe, however, that the fullness of the apostolic communion 'has always to be manifested more fully, and this in company with all other Christians at work in the world'.[15]

Primacy

The nature of primacy in the exercise of ecclesial authority has been one of the major themes of the Vienna consultations. No consensus has been reached on this pertinent question. Both sides have simply reaffirmed their respective understanding of primacy with particular reference to its locus and role in the life of the church.

1. For the Roman Catholic Church the primacy of the Bishop of Rome has always been one of universal dimension and scope, while the Oriental Orthodox Churches have historically practised only a regional primacy.[16]

2. For the Roman Catholic Church the primacy of the Bishop of Rome has 'its roots in the divine plan for the Church', while for the Oriental Orthodox it is only of 'historical origin', and only in the few cases it was confirmed by ecumenical councils.[17]

3. In the Roman Catholic Church the primacy of the Bishop of Rome is formulated and dogmatized. The Oriental Orthodox Churches have never felt such a necessity.[18]

4. For the Roman Catholic Church the infallibility of the church is inseparably connected with the primacy of the Bishop of Rome. For the Oriental Orthodox Churches it is the ecumenical council that manifests the infallibility of the church.[19]

The papal primacy is the natural corollary of the 'pyramidal' concept of the church according to which the pope stands at the top of the communion of local churches: 'The Roman Pontiff, as the successor of Peter, is the perpetual and visible source and foundation of the unity of the bishops and of the multitude of the faithful'.[20] Through its concept of collegiality aimed at the restoration of the authority of the episcopate, Vatican II did attempt to reduce the absolute power of the pope. But the power given to episcopate was quite limited and it was totally conditioned by its head who 'as Vicar of Christ and Pastor of the whole Church... has full, supreme and universal power over the Church. And he can always exercise this power freely.'[21] It is evident that the role of the episcopal college is simply of an advisory nature. The pope is the locus of supreme authority in the Roman Catholic Church.

The position of the Oriental Orthodox Churches can be summarized in this way:

1. The ecumenical council as *consensus fidelium* is the supreme authority in the church. But the ecumenical council is not over the church. Its authority is always subordinate to that of the church.

2. The identification of the Petrine office with the Church of Rome cannot be substantiated biblically or historically. It is due to the development of Western ecclesiology.

3. The juridical and centralized interpretation of Petrine pre-eminence is not acceptable either. The Petrine office cannot be the centre of authority in the church, but only a symbol of unity. The important distinction that Hans Küng makes between 'the necessity for a centre in the Church, and papal centralism, between the necessity for the Petrine office, and papalism',[22] in my view could be an acceptable basis for a real fecclesiological convergence between our churches.

4. The bearer of authority in the church is the college of bishops.

The ministerial power was entrusted by Christ to the apostles collectively and not to a single apostle. It is in the name of the entire episcopate that a local bishop consecrates a bishop. The family of the Oriental Orthodox Churches maintains first that the authority in the church should be exercised by all the bishops together, in fellowship with the head of the episcopal college and not under the head. Secondly, with the same argument, a single bishop cannot be the visible principle of 'universal' unity. It is the *collegium episcoporum*, as successor to the college of apostles, that constitutes the visible sign of communion between local churches.

5. Neither the Petrine office nor the ecumenical council can be regarded by the Oriental Orthodox Churches as indispensable for the manifestation of the unity of the church. The eucharist is the sole basis and structure of the unity of the church. The Petrine office, in my view, may play an important role in the growth of unity, if it first undergoes a deep transformation and become conciliar in its nature, through the decentralization of its authority, a genuine exercise of collegiality, and recognition of the legitimate autonomy of local churches. It may also promote unity if it is conceived in terms of 'service structure' rather than 'power structure'.

The ecumenical councils

The Vienna consultations have also discussed the place and role of the ecumenical council in the life of the church. Three major points have emerged as consensus:

◇ The church as a *koinonia* is a conciliar gathering. Conciliarity is integral to the nature of the church. It is important, however, to distinguish between the council as an 'event', and conciliarity as an 'aspect' of the life of the church.[23]

◇ The ecumenical council is not a permanent structure of the church. It is convoked in response to a specific and urgent situation. Therefore, holding ecumenical councils at given intervals is not a necessity.[24]

◇ As to the anathemata, the general agreement was that first, the acceptance of those anathematized as teachers or saints by the churches who formally condemned them was neither fair nor obligatory. Secondly, a formal lifting of anathemas by both sides was not necessary. This may be done gradually and informally.[25]

It has not been possible to reach a *modus vivendi* on the following two subjects: the ecumenicity and reception of councils (three, seven or twenty-one), and the role of the Bishop of Rome in the council.

It is worth making a few observations, from an Orthodox perspective, concerning the points mentioned above:

The church is always conciliar in or outside an ecumenical council.

Therefore, because of its conciliar nature, it is neither necessary nor obligatory for the church to have regular ecumenical councils, since it can express its conciliarity otherwise than through an ecumenical council. Conciliarity and not the ecumenical council is a vital dimension of the church's life. The councils were *ad hoc* meetings to deal with concrete problems of an emergency nature. The history of the church does not recognize any permanent need or a structure for a regular ecumenical council. The very fact that the Oriental Orthodox Churches, since 431, and the Eastern Orthodox Churches, since 787, continued their life and witness without ecumenical councils is highly significant in this respect. Even the 'General Councils' of the Roman Catholic Church were not regular gatherings. They were emergency meetings held to cope with urgent issues of a given period.

For the Oriental Orthodox Churches the first three ecumenical councils constitute the crux of the apostolic faith.

Other councils did not add anything substantial to the teachings of Nicea (325), Constantinople (381) and Ephesus (431). All later creeds and conciliar decisions may be seen as attempts to elaborate the fundamental truth expressed in the Nicene Creed. It is a fact that the first three ecumenical councils express a more complete vision because of their more general acceptance in the church.[26] Therefore not all the councils of the church should be taken with the same value and significance. The principle of a certain 'hierarchy of truths' should be applied in evaluating the importance of the councils. We believe that there are good reasons to identify the first three ecumenical councils as being indispensable and crucial for our common tradition. Theologically speaking it is very difficult, if not impossible, for the Oriental Orthodox to attribute any ecumenical significance and binding character to the rest of the ecumenical-councils.

The Oriental Orthodox Churches consider the ecumenical council as the supreme authority in the church.
The prerogatives of the pope in the council as they are defined by *codex iuris canonici*[27] and later reaffirmed by Vatican II, are not acceptable for us. The role of the Bishop of Rome needs to be seen within the council and not above it, although we do consider the concept of collegiality of Vatican II a positive step taken in the right direction.[28] In our opinion, neither the head of a local church, even if he enjoys some kind of pre-eminence in the conciliar fellowship of the local churches, nor the geographical representation nor the composition nor the teachings of a council can determine its authority and ecumenicity. They emerge from the *consensus fidelium*.

Chalcedonian Christology

Chalcedonian Christology has occupied an important place on the agenda of our discussions. An agreement has been reached on the following points:

◇ The same apostolic tradition was affirmed as the 'common basis' of our faith.[29]

◇ The decisions and teachings of Nicea, Constantinople and Ephesus were accepted by both Churches.[30]

◇ The Nestorian and Eutychian teachings were rejected as heresies.[31]

◇ Jesus Christ was confessed as being perfect in his divinity and perfect in his humanity. The divine and human natures of Christ are united without confusion, mixture, division and separation.[32]

◇ The existing differences in theological formulations, interpretations and emphasizes have to be understood in the light of Nicea and Constantinople.[33]

◇ The mystery of Christ remains inexhaustible and ineffable. It transcends human perceptions and expressions. Constant and common efforts need to be made to have a more comprehensive grasp of this mystery.[34]

In fact, our common faith in the apostolic kerygma, our common commitment to the tradition of the one church, our common attachment to the Trinitarian-incarnational mystery of Christ and our common Niceno-Constantinopolitan theological heritage constitute the firm ground and the proper context of our Christology.

Having said this, the Oriental Orthodox Churches maintain unequivocally that:

1. The first three ecumenical councils are the foundation of our Christology, and, as such, they cannot be altered or added to. Chalcedon is only an interpretation of Nicea and Constantinople. The Chalcedonian formula is not a *credo* but only a theological statement.

2. The *physis* of Christ is both human and divine with all the properties of the two natures without mixture, confusion or separation. The human and divine natures do not act separately, but always together, inseparably united in one person. The hypostatic union of two natures makes them one. They are separated in thought alone: 'We confess the oneness of two natures'[35] which, in fact, is not a numerical one, but a united one.

3. Terminology remains a major problem in Christology. Chalcedonian controversies proved that the same terms and formulations often had different meanings and implications in different cultural and theological contexts. Chalcedon affirmed '*en duo*' out of fear of Eutychianism. The Oriental Orthodox Churches held firm '*ek duo*' over against the Nestorian tendency. Two sides used different terminologies for different concerns. Their intention, however, was the same: to maintain intact the teachings of the first three ecumenical councils against the invasion of Nestorianism. The words of Nerses the Gracious, a twelfth-century Armenian theologian are, indeed, challenging: 'If "one nature" is said for the indivisible and indissoluble union, and not for the confusion; and "two natures" as being unconfused, immutable and indivisible, both are within the bounds of Orthodoxy.'[36]

Historical and cultural factors are still predominant in our Christological thinking. We are still expressing the one faith that we confess in different ways and with different emphases. One cannot ignore these realities. In our common attempt to reach a full consensus in Christology, and reappropriate our respective Christological teachings for our own times, I believe that we need to take seriously into consideration the following:

◇ First, the Chalcedonian Christology and the reaction of Oriental Orthodox Churches to it must be interpreted in its proper historical background and theological milieu.

◇ Secondly, any given terminology should not be taken as being exclusive, perfect or exhaustive. The mystery can never be wholly grasped by the human mind nor fully expressed by any human verbal utterance. We have to look for a consensus in the very substance of faith and not in its formulation.

◇ Thirdly, it is important that we transcend the Chalcedonian terminology as a verbal expression of concepts, and identify its real intention, making it relevant to modern patterns of thinking and realities of life. This is where we actually are.

The Vienna consultations rendered a great service to our churches in terms of bringing in focus those theological areas and concerns that we have in common as well as identifying those issues that still separate us. We must give thanks to God that in spite of centuries-old controversies that deeply affected the life and hampered the efficiency of the witness of our churches, we are still able to stand together on the common ground of apostolic faith and tradition which, in fact, constitute the very source of our unity in Christ. What has been achieved through Pro Oriente so far makes us hopeful. There are still serious problems of ecclesiological, dogmatic, canonical and jurisdictional natures that need to be wrestled with constantly, and with an ecumenical spirit.

Four consultations cannot settle the problems and misunderstandings that have been accumulated in the course of a long history. The continuation of this process of critical reflection is vitally important. This is our common ecumenical calling which is more urgent today than at any time. It is beyond the immediate purview of this presentation to propose guidelines for our future work together. I would venture only to make a few suggestions:

1. The findings of the four Vienna consultations have not yet been formally assessed by our churches. Nor are they widely known to many even in the clergy. These consultations were talks exclusively among theologians, and they remained so. It is absolutely important that first, Pro Oriente finds proper ways and means to secure a wider circulation of the results of these consultations, both among the clergy and the laity. The publication of the *Selection of the Papers and Minutes of the Four Vienna Consultations*[37] by Pro Oriente only recently, and its translation into Arabic are, indeed, significant steps in this respect. Secondly, our churches need to evaluate seriously, at

various levels—through synodical committees, theological faculties, seminaries, study groups and so on—the convergent and divergent points in our theological teachings that were quite explicitly spelled out in these theological dialogues.

2. The consensus reached in the Vienna consultations on various issues ought not to be taken in exclusive terms. These are still open questions. They need to be further deepened and elucidated as well as constantly tested against the background of our historical experiences and in the light of our respective theological teachings and ecclesiological assumptions. In other words, any superficial and hasty evaluation of the findings of these encounters might have its negative repercussions on the future of our dialogue.

3. As we continue our theological dialogue with a more organized programme and well-studied agenda, we must not aim only for a consensus formula or *modus vivendi* on issues that separate us; rather we have to seek and strengthen together our common roots in the apostolic tradition. The unity of the church is not only a theological agreement, but essentially a continuous growth in the apostolic tradition.

4. The insights and experiences that we have gained from the previous meetings should lead us to address ourselves more boldly to critical and sensitive issues. It is also important that we revise the style, the methodology and the representation of Pro Oriente consultations. I would suggest that a joint and permanent committee be appointed to organize consultations and study seminars, and look after the implementation of their recommendations.

5. We tackled mostly dogmatic issues. We must now deal with pastoral questions and the kind of problems and concerns that touch the life and mission of our churches in their local situations. We ought to know more about each other. We have to learn more from each other through personal encounters, visitation programmes, and co-operation before we engage our churches formally in this process. The ecumenical collaboration on the local level is of crucial importance for the enhancement of our dialogue on the global level. Close collaboration in *diakonia*, inter-church aid, pastoral concerns, theological education, social issues and other matters of a practical nature is indispensable. Combating proselytism must remain a top priority on our agenda.

6. The ongoing bilateral talks between the Roman Catholic Church and some of the Oriental Orthodox Churches, in my opinion, cannot be regarded as an appropriate structure for a formal dialogue. You have to deal with us as a family. On our part we need to have, as a family, one theological stand on the issues that still separate us. Such an approach on both sides may immensely facilitate our dialogue. Bilateral dialogues are important, indeed. They help us to identify our common teachings and scrutinize, in a much more serious way, our respective positions and views. But bilateral dialogues should not be separated from multilateral dialogues. They are interdependent dimensions of the ecumenical fellowship. What the four Vienna consultations achieved is only a beginning—a promising and challenging one, indeed. The aim of Pro Oriente should not be just 'to promote mutual understanding of the Christians in the East and the Christians in the West',[38] but also and fundamentally to bring its important share to the common search for visible unity among all the churches.

We have come a long way. But the road to unity is long, thorny and costly. Let us continue to be faithful and committed pilgrims of this sacred road.

Notes

1. Four unofficial theological consultations (7–12 September, 1971; 3–9 September, 1973; 30 August–5 September, 1976 and 11–17 September, 1978) have taken place between theologians of the Oriental Orthodox Churches and the Roman Catholic Church in Vienna, Austria by the invitation of Pro Oriente, an ecumenical foundation of the Catholic Archdiocese of Vienna.

2. After fifteen centuries of separation caused by the Council of Chalcedon (451), the official bilateral dialogue between the Oriental and Eastern Orthodox Churches started in 1986, and since then, the representatives of these Churches met twice in Chambesy, Switzerland and produced a consensus document on Christology. The said document has already been submitted to the heads of the churches for study and reaction.

3. *Wort und Wahrheit*, supplementary issue number 3, 1976, page 223. The papers and the ensuing discussions together with the communiqués of the four consultations have appeared in four supplementary issues of the same review: number 1, 1972; number 2, 1974; number 3, 1976; number 4, 1978. This review which is published by Pro Oriente will be referred to as *WW* plus the number of the issue.

4.   Ibid.

5.   *WW* 4, page 233.

6.   In the New Testament the church is identified with the eucharistic assembly of a particular place. The concept of the local church was then developed from 'polis' to 'metropolis', and later to a church of a particular nation. In Protestant ecclesiology, by local church is generally meant the local congregation, namely, the parish. Both in Orthodox and Catholic ecclesiology, by local church is generally meant the episcopal diocese. In the Roman Catholic ecclesiology the 'local church' has been sometimes used interchangeably with *ecclesia particularis* which implies a wider geographical locality and contains several dioceses.

7.   Walter M. Abbott, *The Documents of Vatican II*, translated by J. Gallagher, Geoffrey Chapman, 1966, page 50.

8.   Ibid., page 44.

9.   Ibid., pages 22–23.

10. Ibid., page 34.

11. Ibid., page 44.

12. Ibid., page 32.

13. *Ecumenical Collaboration at the Regional, National and Local Levels*, Vatican, 1980, page 19.

14. I use the 'Orthodox Church' in its broader sense comprising both the Oriental and Eastern families of Orthodox tradition.

15. 'The Struggle for Justice and the Unity of the Church: Crete, May 7–14, 1975' in *Orthodox Contribution to Nairobi*, compiled and presented by the Orthodox Task Force of the WCC, WCC, 1975, page 31.

16. *WW* 4, page 232.

17. Ibid., page 233.

18. Ibid.

19. Ibid.

20. Walter M. Abbott, *The Documents of Vatican II*, translated by J. Gallagher, Geoffrey Chapman, 1966, page 44.

21. Ibid., page 43.

22. Hans Küng, *The Council in Action: Theological Reflection on the Second Vatican Council*, Sheed and Ward, 1963, page 64.

23. *WW* 3, page 223.

24. Ibid.

25. *WW* 2, page 176.

26. Ibid., *WW* 3, page 223.

27. See canon 222.

28. *WW* 2, page 176.

29. *WW* 1, page 182; *WW* 2, pages 175–76.

30. *WW* 1, page 182; *WW* 2, page 175.

31. *WW* 1, page 182; *WW* 2, page 176.

32. *WW* 1, page 182; *WW* 2, pages 176-77.

33. Ibid.

34. Ibid.

35. *Universal Encyclical of St. Nerses the Gracious*, Etchmiadzine, 1865, page 91 (in Armenian).

36. Ibid., page 97.

37. *Selection of the Papers and Minutes of the Four Vienna Consultations*, Pro Oriente, 1988. The Arabic translation of this volume has been published in 1991 in Damascus.

38. Ibid., page 7.

8

Unity and Mission in the
Context of the Middle East

A paper read to the Plenary Commission on
Faith and Order, Budapest, Hungary, 1989.[1]

I have been asked to offer to this meeting of the Plenary Commission on Faith and Order a Middle-Eastern perspective on the question of the interrelatedness of unity and mission. In order to proceed with some clarity and order, I would like to raise four questions: Why is this item on the agenda of Faith and Order? How is the interrelatedness of unity and mission manifested in the life and witness of the churches in the Middle East? What are the implications of this interconnectedness with reference to the future work of Faith and Order? Let me try to provide some answers to these questions, with particular reference to the third.

Background to the discussion

The concern for a dynamic interrelation between unity and mission has been, during the last ten years, a growing trend in the life and work of the World Council of Churches in general, and in Faith and Order and the Commission on World Mission and Evangelism (CWME) in particular. In fact the issue as such is not a new one for the WCC. In 1951, in the so-called Rolle declaration about the interrelation of unity and mission, the WCC emphatically stated that they are 'indissolubly connected'.[2]

This basic theological conviction, however, was never given any significant expression in the programmes of the council. For example, one could hardly identify the question of mission in Faith and Order's continuous search for visible unity, or the question of unity in the programmatic concerns of CWME. Although some attempts of limited scope were made to spell out the important aspects and implications of the interconnectedness of unity and mission, they basically remained separate issues and underwent parallel theological developments in the thought and work of the council at large.

As you know, during the last few years, upon the recommendation of the WCC Executive Committee (1984), a joint project on unity and mission was launched by Faith and Order and CWME with an aim of holding a world conference on unity and mission. Later on, upon the insistence of Faith and Order, it was decided to cancel the joint world conference and initiate a 'joint theological reflection and clarification of the interrelation between mission and unity' to help the churches 'to integrate these two concerns in their faith and witness'.[3] It was also agreed that this process of common theological exploration should culminate with a joint statement to be presented to the next assembly of the WCC in Canberra (1991). As a first step towards a programmatic cooperation, some preliminary efforts were made by both sides to reread 'Baptism, Eucharist and Ministry' and 'Mission and Evangelism: An Ecumenical Affirmation' in their interrelatedness. The outcome of this rather experimental attempt was, in my judgment, significant in opening a promising avenue for possible future joint work between Faith and Order and CWME in this area.

Just a few months ago, CWME, at its San Antonio world conference, came up with a strong affirmation that mission and unity belong together. In my view, a joint statement on unity and mission could be only the immediate aim of this joint venture. We have to go beyond that, and I think even beyond the 'joint theological reflection and clarification', to embark on a process of programmatic collaboration with CWME. Therefore in this meeting we, as the Commission on Faith and Order, are invited to pursue the discussion with an attempt to outline, at least in its major elements, the content, the nature, and the scope of our joint work with CWME.

Unity and mission: one act of one church

The *raison d'être* of the church includes two inseparable dimensions: unity in Christ and service to humanity. Unity points to what the church is to be and mission to what the church has to do. In fact, the church is not only a community that grows into communion with Christ but also a community that is being sent by Christ to the world with a specific mission. One should not, therefore, speak only in terms of interaction or interrelation, but of the intimate interwovenness of unity and mission. To draw a line of demarcation between the two is simply a new heresy. A divided church cannot have a united mission. Mission without unity is void of any ecclesiological basis.

But what do we mean by 'unity' and 'mission'? These questions are not directly related to my topic. However, let me, as an Orthodox coming from the Middle East, open here a parenthesis and give you some brief and simple answers to these rather complex questions.

1. The unity of the church is neither a doctrinal *modus vivendi* nor merely co-operation nor a kind of peaceful co-habitation. It is the communion of the church in Christ as well as the communion of local churches in one faith and one eucharistic fellowship. The church is one 'in each place' and 'in all places'.[4]

2. The church itself has no mission. Its mission is to participate in God's mission. The very being of the church is missionary; the church is, indeed, a missionary event. Therefore, mission is not one of the 'functions' of the church, but the life of the church that goes beyond itself to embrace the whole of humanity and the whole creation. The mission of the church is not the expansion of the church, but the establishment of the kingdom of God. Unity and mission must be understood in the perspective of the kingdom. They are for the kingdom and, as such, they are dynamically interrelated.[5]

What does this mean? The interrelatedness of unity and mission is not a question of methodology or strategy. It is an ontologial one. It is related to the very essence of *koinonia* as fellowship in the Triune God, and to the specific vocation of *koinonia* as participation in God's economy in and for the world. In fact 'being in Christ' (a favourite expression of Paul) is being a partner in his work. Therefore unity is participation in the life of the Triune God. Mission is commitment to the work of the Triune God incarnated in Jesus Christ. Both are God's gift and command. It is only in unity with the Triune God that the church is able to fulfill its vocation.

Unity is a pre-condition for mission. Co-operation in mission can enhance unity. Unity in its turn cannot be considered as an independent concern. It has to be located in the context of God's saving purpose for all humanity, for the whole creation. Thus the 'departmentalization' of unity and mission is a distortion of the true nature of the church. Therefore the question of whether to have 'mission and unity' or 'unity and mission' which prevailed at a certain time in our ecumenical discussion is, in my view, a false dichotomy. In the praxis of the early church there was never such a separation or prioritizing. Unity and mission have always belonged to the very essence of the church. The call to unity and the call to mission have never been different callings, but always one call; not different acts, but always one act of one church. Each one was conditioned and determined by the other; each one led into the other.

Unity and mission are for the upbuilding (*oikodome*) of the church in its commitment to God's purpose for the world. But the interrelatedness referred to above remains only a theory if it is not given concrete expression in the life of the community of faith. The churches are constantly challenged to reread the biblical message and to listen to the call of God for unity and mission in different socio-economic and politico-religious contexts.[6] In fact, the credibility of *ecclesia* depends on how it responds to the call of God in Christ and participates in his work.

Unity and mission in the Middle East

In the Middle East the churches are striving for visible unity and a common mission in the context of multi-religious societies and in the midst of ideological conflicts and turmoil.[7] To the best of my knowledge, unity and mission are not presented to the churches in any part of the world with such acute urgency—indeed as the only option for survival—as in the Middle East. They are integral to, and closely interconnected with the daily life and witness of our churches. In what way is the interrelatedness of unity and mission presently manifested in the actual life of the churches in the Middle East? What are its most distinctive features? An elaborate analysis of this issue is beyond the purview of my presentation. I will try, within the space allotted to me, to bring under the spotlight only those aspects which, I believe, not only illustrate the inseparable and dynamic interconnection of unity and mission, but also help us to have a comprehensive and correct grasp of the peculiarity of the Middle East within world Christendom.

1. EUCHARIST: THE EMERGING AND CONVERGING POINT OF UNITY AND MISSION

The eucharist is the source of unity and mission. In the eucharist, they become one act of the church. In other words, in the eucharistic celebration, the community of faith is not only united with Christ, but also sent to the world by Christ. It is this eucharistic fellowship with Christ that constitutes the very foundation of mission. It is this sending out to the world that sustains and gives concrete implications to unity with Christ. The eucharistic act is, by its very nature, an act of unity and mission. It is both the ingoing (*missio ad intra*) and the outgoing (*missio ad extra*) of the church.

The interrelatedness of unity and mission is given a dynamic manifestation in the eucharist. Eating the body and drinking the blood of Christ makes us one with Christ, transforms us into new people of the new creation and sends us to the world to transform and re-create it through Christ: 'For as often as you eat this bread and drink this cup, you proclaim the Lord's death until he comes' (1 Corinthians 11:26).

The eucharist is a sharing event. God shares himself with us, entering into our life and making us one with him. At the same time God invites us to share in his divinity. This mutual sharing of God and humanity is aimed at the salvation of humanity and creation. In fact, sharing one bread means sharing one mission and vice versa. The eucharist is the communion of the community of faith in the life and fellowship of the Triune God. It is, as well, participation in God's mission in the world through the proclamation of the good news, service to one's neighbour and the struggle against dehumanizing structures and powers. Therefore any step towards unity and engagement in mission is essentially a eucharistic act. It is through the eucharist that the church becomes *koinonia* in the Triune God. It is through the eucharist act that *koinonia* becomes a 'missionary event'[8] acquiring kergymatic and diaconic functions.

The eucharist is a sign of, as well as a call for, unity and mission. It is the kingdom in anticipation, and as such it embraces the whole of creation. Local and universal, time and space are united in it. The eucharist as the supreme manifestation of unity and mission has always been at the heart of Christian life in the Middle East. The eucharist has built up the community of faith and sustained it in its life and witness. In the past, during the times of persecution, and today, in a minority situation, the eucharist remains for our churches the living source as well as the emerging and converging point of unity and mission.

2. UNITY AND MISSION AS A CONTINUOUS *DIAKONIA*

Diakonia belongs to the very nature of the church. Being in communion with Christ is loving one's neighbour, being with the sick and afflicted. These are not just the 'moral obligations' of the church but rather its constitutive elements. The church does not 'have' a *diakonia*; it is a *diakonia*, namely a continuous and committed discipleship to Christ for the rebuilding of world community and re-creating the fallen world according to the plans of God. Through *diakonia* the church becomes one with Christ and at the same time brings Christ to the world. *Diakonia* is both the expression of the unity of the church and the implementation of the gospel message.

Such an understanding of *diakonia* has always been dominant in the life of the churches in the Middle East. It has been a living source of growth in unity and an effective way of witnessing to Christ. Our churches have developed a kind of *diakonia* that goes beyond regular charity and expresses the basic values of Christian faith and life through sharing, solidarity and community building. The churches' *diakonia* has gone beyond the confessional and Christian boundaries to include the Muslim society at large. In fact the churches' diaconic role, particularly in the areas of health, welfare and education, has become a driving force in the development of social action in the multi-religious societies of the Middle East.

Diakonia has also introduced division and mistrust in the region. The flow of Western *diakonia* to the area through Western structures and methodologies has not only created a strong dependency between the so-called 'receiving' and the 'donor' churches and brought about divisions among the local churches, but also has become a factor of mistrust among the Muslim societies vis-à-vis the local churches. The return to a local, indigenous *diakonia* remains a basic bond of fellowship among the local churches, an important instrument of Christian mission and a safe avenue of good relations with our neighbours. During the last few decades our churches have taken significant and promising steps to this effect, particularly through the creation of the Middle East Council of Churches and other local ecumenical bodies.

3. UNITY AND MISSION AS SOLIDARITY WITH THE OPPRESSED

Being in the fellowship of the Triune God and proclaiming the gospel both call for a firm attitude towards the situation of injustice. The church exists for the kingdom, it serves the kingdom. It cannot become and remain a eucharistic community—the sign, the foretaste and sacrament of the kingdom—without entering into the brokenness of the world and facing violence, hatred, injustice and evil. Therefore, any attempt to separate unity and mission from social justice would be a denial of the true nature of the church.

The church has a prominent role to play. This implies judging the world, rejecting its 'principalities and powers', challenging human self-confidence and self-sufficiency, and taking sides with the oppressed. This is an inseparable part of the church's unity and mission. Solidarity with the poor and oppressed has been central to the life and witness of the churches in the Middle East. Our churches have always been amongst the avant-garde in movements of liberation, nationalization, anti-colonialism and in the struggle for human rights and self-determination. In fact, the churches' aware-ness of their common responsibility vis-à-vis justice and peace has helped immensely in giving more visibility to their unity, as well as a meaningful and efficient expression to Christian mission in the multi-religious societies of the Middle East.

4. UNITY AND MISSION AS A CALL FOR RENEWAL

The Christ-event is a call for a new relationship with God and the world. This call becomes a reality in the eucharist which is the new creation. Thus the church is not a participant in the renewal process of the world; it is a community renewed by and in Christ, and is destined to become the ferment of, and instrument for, the renewal of the whole of humanity and creation. Therefore mission is not the expansion of the church, an overseas 'enterprise', but essentially the renewal of the local community of faith[9] for the renewal of the entire human community.

The unity of the church is not a doctrinal consensus, but fundamentally the renewal of broken fellowship with Christ. The unity of the church and humankind, and the renewal of the church and the world, are inseparably linked in the divine economy. Renewal is thus a dynamic process of becoming what God intended to do for the world in Jesus Christ. It is never simply a change[10] in response to new conditions, but essentially the transformation of human beings, community and the whole creation.

Renewal is an urgent 'must' for the churches of the Middle East. The self-purification and self-understanding of these churches through a dynamic process of critical self-assessment is, indeed, a growing need. In my view, our churches must be involved in this renewal process on three interconnected levels:

First, our churches should re-Christianize those areas of their life where secularization has become dominant to the extent of questioning the viability and reliability of Christian faith. Education, youth work, women and family life are crucial domains where the church can and must enhance the renewal process.

Secondly, Middle-Eastern Christianity must 're-orientalize' itself, that is, it must re-discover and express anew its Eastern roots and identity. The overwhelming presence of Western norms of life, categories of thinking, and structures and methodologies of decision-making in the life of these churches has not only begun to distort their own identity but also led them to be considered, in some sensitive regions, as so-called 'representatives' of Western cultures and ideologies. Therefore a process of critical indigenization is an absolute necessity for the restoration of true identity, as well as for the acceptability of these churches by their Muslim neighbours.

Thirdly, the churches of the Middle East are more sensitive to their obedience to the past than concerned with the new demands and the growing concerns of present-day societies. They are called to discern, through a creative process of self-renewal, the challenges of the kingdom in the midst of new and often conflicting situations. Renewal is a progress towards unity. It is, as well, an obedient response to God's call for the salvation of the world. The words of the heads of the churches in the Middle East are quite eloquent: 'Unless we live in a constant state of spiritual renewal ... we will be unable to give a vital witness.'[11]

5. UNITY AND MISSION AS DIALOGUE IN A MULTI-RELIGIOUS SOCIETY

Our relationship with God and our mission to the world cannot be separated from our relationship with our neighbour. In the pluralistic societies of today 'my neighbour's faith and mine'[12] do not simply co-exist; they interact and correlate. In fact, we always remind ourselves in our ecumenical pilgrimage that the unity of the church and the unity of humankind are interdependent and that there exists a growing interaction between the living faiths. We have also come to realize that the transformation of the world and the building of world community are no longer a one-way track. It implies mutual openness, mutual listening and a common partnership.

Unity and mission are wrestled with in the Middle East exclusively in the context of dialogue with Islam.[13] Dialogue in this part of the world is not a conceptual notion but an existential reality. It is a way of life, one which has penetrated into all spheres of society. The churches lie in a situation of permanent dialogue. They share with Islam the same land, the same history and the same destiny. The daily encounter with Islam has greatly affected our theological outlook, our values and traditions, our understanding of ourselves; in other words, the whole existence of the churches is shaped by their living among Muslims.

The Christian mission in the Middle East is not aimed at the conversion of Islam. We are living with people who are different in many respects and intend to remain different. But neither can the churches abandon their mission and replace it by dialogue. Thus they virtually live in a dilemma. On the one hand, their minority situation forces the churches to adopt a defensive attitude towards Islam; and on the other hand, the present-day demands and concerns of common interest challenge the churches to live and witness in a context of continuous dialogical interaction with Islam.

It is my firm conviction that it is high time for our churches to discover new missionary potentials. Such an approach might sound somewhat doubtful, particularly at this present juncture of the history of the Middle East where the churches are directly faced with the resurgence of Muslim fundamentalism. But, in my judgment, there are at least three ways through which Christian unity and mission can be given a new stimulus and manifestation.

◇ First, the minority situation should not lead our churches to a state of stagnation and isolation, but must rather engage them in a dynamic process of spiritual renewal. If it is conceived in the right perspective, and practised in a creative way, renewal is a source of strength and self-confidence.

◇ Secondly, the resurgence of Muslim radicalism means the rejection of secular and technological cultures, Western traditions and norms. It means the search for a spiritual basis for life.[14] In spite of its negative repercussions the revival of Islam can be taken, in a sense, as a positive development and can become an encouraging factor in the churches' search for their true identity in Christ.

◇ Thirdly, the criterion and perspectives which we used in the past to deal with Islam are no longer valid today. We need a coherent and relevant theology to make us more reliable partners to our neighbours in our common mission for world community-building. We need a new theology which must be strong enough to open to 'mutual witness'[15] while resisting any temptation leading towards a possible compromise.

6. UNITY AND MISSION: *SINE QUA NON* FOR SURVIVAL

The church is a living reality in time and space. Hence, the church cannot live out its unity and carry on its mission without continuity. The question of continuity is of crucial importance for the churches in the Middle East. Having been located as a tiny community in a predominantly Muslim socio-cultural milieu, the churches are permanently exposed to the danger of losing their distinct identity. In fact the politico-military upheavals, the economic instability and other prevailing negative factors and aspects have considerably reduced the physical presence of Christianity and the effectiveness of Christian witness in the region. It is a plain fact that the very survival of the churches in the Middle East is at stake today more than at any time in their history.

This is a major concern, one of utmost urgency and priority. The question of unity and mission is, in fact, a question of survival. For the centuries-old churches of the region, survival is never just continuity, barren existence or self-perpetuation. It is faithfulness to the past, openness to new realities, courage for renewal and commitment to unity and mission. Our churches should be con-sciously aware of the fact that they cannot secure their continuity, and maintain their proper identity, without visible unity and a common mission. The present situation of the Middle East makes the imperative of unity and mission much more acute and urgent.

7. UNITY AND MISSION AS A 'MINISTRY OF RECONCILIATION'

The unity that Christ prayed for to his Father was not only the communion of the church with God, but also the communion of the whole of humanity with God. The mission of the church is to prepare and anticipate the way towards the unity of the whole of humanity and of the whole created order through the incorporation of 'all things' in Christ. God 'through Christ reconciled us to himself' and gives us 'the ministry of reconciliation' (2 Corinthians 5:18). We are, therefore, 'ambassadors for Christ' bringing 'the message of reconciliation' (2 Corinthians 5:19–20). The church can achieve its God-given mandate only by taking tangible steps towards visible unity and common witness.

The 'ministry of reconciliation' is a major aim of the churches' unity and mission in the Middle East where ideological and political confrontations, manifested often through military clashes as well as structures of injustice and oppression, prevail with ever more acuteness and destruction. Our churches are called to become the sign of hope in a situation of profound hopelessness, the foretaste of the kingdom *vis-à-vis* the predominance of 'principalities and powers', the instrument of unity and reconciliation in the midst of growing tensions and polarization. The churches are partners with their Muslim neighbours in a common struggle for the rebuilding of Middle-Eastern society on the basis of God's justice and peace, of human rights and dignity.

8.   UNITY AND MISSION AS A LIVING *MARTURIA*

I already pointed out that unity is a fellowship in the life of the Triune God and mission is participation in the work of God in the world. Unity and mission belong to God. The church is only an agent. It is God himself, in Jesus Christ, who is present and acts in the church's continuous struggle for unity and mission. Therefore, commitment to unity and engagement in mission is a costly discipleship. It is a living *marturia*.

In fact, *marturia* is the highest expression of the unity of the church and the most concrete sign of the authenticity of Christian mission. *Marturia* is not only bodily suffering or death; it is that quality of life and witness which makes the gospel message an incarnational reality in the midst of the tensions and suffering of the world. Endeavour for unity and involvement in mission have been, for the churches of the Middle East, a continuous *marturia* in life and even in death. This has been due not only to the historical circumstances which they went through, and the present hard realities to which they are exposed, but to an ecclesiology which considers unity and mission in terms of sacramental vision. In the present situation of the Middle East, and *vis-à-vis* the enormous difficulties there of such varied nature and scope, the very existence of these churches is, indeed, a living *marturia*.

A few remarks on Faith and Order and CWME collaboration

The concerns and perspectives emerging from the Christian presence and witness in the Middle East point in an existential way to the interconnectedness of unity and mission. Undoubtedly, this interconnectedness acquires much more visibility and urgency in the context of a multi-religious society. The Middle East is only one concrete example of that; we have many more or less similar situations in different parts of the world where Christian unity and mission are manifested in their intimate interrelationship. In fact, the barriers and boundaries that used to separate nations and societies have almost disappeared. We are living in an interdependent and pluralistic world. Even so-called 'Christian' Europe has become a pluralistic society. Therefore the present reality of the world urges us to deal with utmost seriousness with the question of unity in a broader ecclesiological perspective, and in relation to issues with which the churches grapple in their missionary involvement.

It also reminds us to conceive of mission as emerging from fellowship in the Triune God and inseparable from the unity of the church. Therefore the interrelatedness of unity and mission is more than a joint 'project' or a programmatic concern. It deals with the very nature of the church. Hence, some sort of working relationship between Faith and Order and CWME is imperative. It is beyond the purview of my task to outline the future work between these two sub-units of the WCC. I would just like to make a few observations in this respect.

In my view, any kind of programmatic collaboration between Faith and Order and CWME must be based on the following criteria:

1. Faith and Order and CWME have different histories, traditions, orientations and styles of work. Faith and Order is a movement; CWME is not. The distinctiveness of these two bodies should be maintained intact. More precisely, Faith and Order must remain Faith and Order. Any compromise in the very identity of this movement or in its various structural, constitutional and programmatic aspects, is simply not acceptable.

2. The desired collaboration should not aim at producing a consensus document, but should seek ways and means of establishing creative interaction between unity and mission. This could be done through various programmes, study processes and work on the crucial issues of Faith and Order and CWME.

3. This joint initiative should eventually help Faith and Order and CWME to see their respective work as converging—and not parallel—processes.

4. Faith and Order needs to see its work not in terms of a study project, but as a dynamic process relating its insights, perspectives and visions to the daily experiences of the local churches. CWME in its action-oriented programmes needs to listen to Faith and Order in order to have a fuller grasp of the nature of Christian faith and truth. They both have to conceive their work in terms of mutual questioning and challenging.[16]

In my opinion whatever we do in Faith and Order has concrete missiological implications, and as such needs to be taken up by CWME and integrated in its programmatic concerns. To be more specific, is our commitment to the 'unity of the church and the renewal of humankind' not a missionary challenge? Is our endeavour to 'explicate the apostolic faith' to the present time not an integral part of the mission of our churches in their local situation? Do our strenuous efforts to involve the churches in a 'reception' process of 'baptism, eucharist and ministry' not have a significant bearing on the mission of the church?

Presently I see two opposite tendencies in Faith and Order which, in fact, have become very obvious in our discussions during the last couple of days here in Budapest. One tendency insists on sticking firmly to the mandate of Faith and Order, and the other advocates broadening the scope of Faith and Order issues and concerns. We have to be aware of the risks involved in these one-sided and biased approaches, for the reasons to which I have just referred.

In Faith and Order we do not deal with issues *per se*, detached from the life and witness of the church. Such an understanding of Faith and Order will be the denial of the very nature and the goals of this movement. But neither can we enlarge our agenda to include issues which have only indirect relevance to the basic objectives of Faith and Order. We have to be selective. Therefore the overall work of Faith and Order and CWME must be conceived, planned and implemented in an interrelated way, namely as a comprehensive whole. This is a major concern before us, which we must take seriously in the years to come.

Notes

1. It is published in T.F. Best, editor, 'The Commission Meeting at Budapest' in *Faith and Order, 1985–1989, Faith and Order* Paper No. 148, WCC, 1990, pages

263–275 and in *International Review of Mission*, volume LXXIX, number 316, October 1990, pages 445–452.

2. 'The Calling of the Church to Mission and to Unity', *Minutes and Reports of the Fourth Meeting of the Central Committee, Rolle, Switzerland*, WCC, 1951, page 66. Cited in *International Review of Mission*, volume LXXII, number 286, April 1983, page 154.

3. *Minutes of the Meeting of the Standing Commission: 1986, Potsdam, GDR, Faith and Order* Paper Number 134, WCC, 1986, page 47.

4. Compare the report of the section on unity, New Delhi assembly, in Lukas Vischer, editor, *A Documentary History of the Faith and Order Movement 1927–1963*, Bethany Press, pages 144–145.

5. In the ecumenical movement, the Orthodox churches came to be known as churches essentially concerned with unity. On the other hand, the Protestant churches came to be recognized as having mission as their main preoccupation. It is time that in our ecumenical fellowship we look at these major concerns in their dynamic interrelatedness.

6. In response to God's call for unity and mission the churches have developed, during the last twenty years, in different situations different theological insights, perspectives and visions which have come to be known under the name of liberation theology, black theology, 'God is dead' theology, feminist theology, theology of hope, and so on. It is significant to note that today we no longer do theology exclusively in confessional terms. Our theology has become largely contextual: it is African, South American, Continental, Middle-Eastern, and so on.

7. For a comprehensive assessment of the presence and writings of the churches in the present day Middle East, see my book *The Christian Witness at the Crossroads in the Middle East*, Beirut, 1980.

8. Eucharistic ecclesiology has newly been given quite an important place in our ecumenical discussion. But the eucharist has not yet been given a proper treatment in our missiology. The latter has laid so much emphasis on evangelism and *diakonia*, with a special concern for the practical aspects of mission, that it has almost neglected the eucharistic dimension. This is a lack which needs to be remedied. It is significant to note that eucharist as a 'missionary event' has recently started to emerge in the ecumenical movement in general and in CWME in particular. This line of thinking must be pursued.

9. Emilio Castro is right when he says that 'now we not only talk about mission in six continents, we know that mission is at home, right in our neighbourhood'. *Sent Free*, Geneva, WCC, 1985, page 14.

10. It is important to note that for the West 'change' is equivalent to progress, while for the East it simply means discontinuity. This is why the churches of the Middle East always use the term 'renewal'.

11. 'Pastoral Message', *MECC Perspectives*, October 1986, numbers 6–7, page 16.

12. The title of a study guide for dialogue published in 1986 by the WCC's sub-unit

on Dialogue: *My Neighbour's Faith—and Mine: Theological Discoveries Through Interfaith Dialogue*, WCC, 1986.

13. For a more elaborate treatment of Christian-Muslim dialogue in the Middle East, see my book *The Christian Witness at the Crossroads in the Middle East*, Beirut, 1980.

14. The rapid growth and expansion of Muslim radicalism is becoming a world-wide phenomenon and an acute problem with far-reaching consequences. The anti-liberal, anti-western and anti-secular attitude of this movement, sometimes manifested by violence, worries many societies and states. The Western democracies and Christian-secular societies are considered by radical Muslims as being spiritually and morally bankrupt. They believe that people cannot be governed by laws they make on their own, but by laws imposed by God (*Sharia*), which they can not change or modify in any case. In my view, Muslim fundamentalism needs careful study and correct understanding through frank dialogue. The churches of the Middle East can play an important role in this respect.

15. The concept of 'mutual witness' was raised in the Mombasa (Kenya) conference on dialogue in 1979 (see *Christian Presence and Witness in Relation to Muslim Neighbours*, WCC, 1981). But it was not, in my view, adequately dealt with. The WCC's sub-unit on Dialogue must explore further the potentialities and promises, as well as the dangers, involved in this concept.

16. I do not agree with the characterization of a CWME paper according to which Faith and Order deals with 'discipline' and CWME with 'action' (see Padmasani J. Gallup, 'The BEM Document from a CWME Perspective', Appendix 14 in *CWME: Minutes of the Meeting of the Commission, Geneva, 5–11 July 1987*, WCC, 1987, page 89). In my view, such a separation between 'discipline' and 'action' is neither possible or in accordance with the very nature of the work of these sub-units.

9

From Participation to Partnership: the Orthodox Churches in the World Council of Churches

An address to the Orthodox Consultation 'The Orthodox Churches and the World Council of Churches', in Chambesy, Switzerland, organized by the Ecumenical Patriarchate, 10–15 September, 1991.

I greet you all with the spirit of Christian love and fellowship. We are not here as representatives of different churches but as members of one and the same family. We give thanks to God that after centuries of separation due to historical circumstances and Christological misunderstandings, we have come now to realize through ecumenical encounters and theological dialogues that we share the same Orthodox tradition, and that we are one in the essence of our Christological teachings. This rediscovery of our common belonging to the same and undivided Orthodoxy which has sustained and enriched our witness throughout history will, undoubtedly, give new dynamism and creativity to the Orthodox ecumenical witness. I would like to express my special thanks to the Ecumenical Patriarchate, the Orthodox Task Force, and the General Secretary of the World Council of Churches, all of whom, in one way or another, have made this consultation possible.

To perceive Orthodoxy as merely a historical phenomenon is to distort it. Orthodoxy is not only a subject to be found in the textbooks of church history. A living and continuous reality, it embraces the whole life of the Orthodox Church in its unbroken continuity with the apostolic church as well as in its spiritual, pastoral, liturgical, and theological dimensions and manifestations. Therefore Orthodoxy is not a heritage that must be maintained untouched and untouchable in the annals of history or within the boundaries of our churches. Orthodoxy is a mark of the church that must be lived out, deepened, and strengthened further. It is a mission that must be carried out. As such, Orthodoxy needs to be constantly appropriated and reappropriated, interpreted and re-interpreted, particularly in the *diaspora*, where the Orthodox Churches are in danger of losing the specific identity, theology and spirituality which make up their ethos.

Today's gathering, which comes at a decisive stage in the history of the ecumenical movement, is a landmark in the history of the Orthodox presence and witness in the WCC. We have come here to explore together the ways and the means of opening Orthodoxy to other traditions, putting it in dialogue with other theological perspectives, and transforming the Orthodox presence in the WCC into a better organized and more dynamic witness. We are faced with a number of basic concerns and major challenges. We must tackle them with serenity, sincerity, and utmost seriousness. We must have a common position on those ecumenical issues and trends that dominate the life and work of the council. We must reach for a common understanding on the nature and vocation of the WCC and the ecumenical vision.

In the context of this understanding of our task, and out of my own ecumenical experience, I would like to make a few observations about some of the basic facts and challenges pertaining to Orthodox witness in the WCC. We should bear in mind two fundamental realities, which, I believe, are crucial for a correct and comprehensive understanding of the particular place and specific role of Orthodoxy in the WCC particularly, and in the ecumenical movement generally:

◇ First, the Orthodox presence in the ecumenical movement is not a recent phenomenon. It did not begin in the early 1960s, when most of the Orthodox Churches formally joined the WCC. Indeed, as early as the beginning of this century, the Orthodox Churches, through patriarchal encyclicals and synodical statements,[1] emphasized the pivotal importance of the ecumenical movement for the unity of the church. Furthermore, Orthodox representatives took part in a number of ecumenical gatherings, particularly in those organized by the Faith and Order and Life and Work movements.

◇ Secondly, while the Protestant West was mainly responsible for the emergence of the ecumenical movement and the formation of the WCC, the Orthodox East provided a broader perspective of the ecumenical vision.

Orthodox membership in the WCC has brought many significant changes in the life, nature, image, and structure of the council. Let me mention succinctly the major ones:

1. While the WCC is still to a large degree Protestant in its way of thinking and Western in its structures, it has acquired through Orthodox participation a broader dimension and scope, becoming truly a world council of churches—a fellowship of churches embracing almost the entire *oikumene.*

2. Orthodoxy's most significant contribution is the introduction of the Trinitarian dimension to the theological discussions as well as to the Basis of the WCC. The Christocentric theology of the council has been largely balanced by a Trinitarian approach.

3. The Orthodox helped Western Protestant theology to rediscover its sacramental ecclesiology, the centrality of spirituality and liturgy in Christian life and mission, and the decisive importance of pneumatology.

4. The Orthodox not only initiated debate on some of the major ecclesiological, Christological and pneumatological themes, they also contributed substantially to the debate. They helped particularly to move forward the convergence processes of two controversial theological issues: Chalcedonian Christology, and the study on Baptism, Eucharist, and Ministry (BEM).

5. The question of visible unity, the base on which the WCC was created, has remained, through the constant reminder and persistence of the Orthodox Churches, a primary concern and a priority item on the agenda of the council, as well as the motivating force behind its programmes and activities. The Orthodox have contributed immeasurably to the efforts of Faith and Order aimed at reaching an ecumenical understanding of the nature and vision of unity.

6. The Orthodox Churches led the WCC to condemn proselytism and to recognize the urgent need to abandon proselytizing activities, especially on a local level. They also played a major part in the process of reviewing and clarifying the various aspects of the

theology and practice of mission and evangelism in different contexts, and in the light of new ecumenical realities.

7. The Orthodox Church has constantly questioned the following trends in the life and thought of the council: 'intercommunion' as a means towards the unity of the church; the transformation of the council (*conseil*) into an ecumenical council (*concile*); the attribution of an ecclesial significance to the WCC; the ordination of women; the attempts to change the terminology of the Bible, the conciliar teachings and dogmatic formulations into an inclusive language, and so on.

8. The Orthodox Churches have consistently called for self-criticism, and stressed the need for mutual questioning and accountability as equal members of the same family committed to the same cause. They have also called for, and actively participated in, the continuous reviewing and re-evaluating of the council's structures, functions, and programmatic priorities.[2]

All the factors and aspects outlined above indicate that Orthodoxy is not, as some tend to depict it, a sort of flavour in the overwhelmingly Protestant structures and atmosphere of the council, but is indeed a living and forceful reality and a major ingredient of the world-wide ecumenical fellowship. It is important that somebody write, and in the near future, the history of the ecumenical witness of Orthodoxy in its manifold aspects and manifestations.

The Orthodox Churches, in their turn, have been enriched by their ecumenical involvement.
Orthodoxy has been impelled constantly to reassess itself, its role, and its vision in *oikumene*. This important dimension of Orthodox ecumenical witness must not be ignored. To this effect at least four aspects deserve our attention:

1. In my judgment, the most important and immediate effect of the ecumenical movement on the Orthodox Churches has been the fact that it has provided the Orthodox with the opportunity to meet churches of other traditions and engage in a sincere dialogue with them. It is highly significant to note that the living encounter with and growing involvement in the ecumenical movement has greatly helped the Eastern and Oriental Orthodox Churches to break down the historical and political factors which had isolated them from each other for many centuries. They recovered, with renewed

consciousness and vision, their common roots: their Orthodoxy.[3]

2. In the sphere of theological methodology and hermeneutics, Orthodox theology has been considerably helped by four focuses of western theology: emphasis on the centrality of the Bible and the kerygma, a critical approach to church history, biblical textual criticism, and the missionary character of theology. Undoubtedly, this creative interaction between Eastern Orthodox and Western Protestant theological methodologies, norms, and perspectives has considerably enriched 'ecumenical theology'.

3. The ecumenical dialogue brought the Orthodox Churches out of their 'national' boundaries and socio-cultural milieu, and engaged them with other churches in a common action on a global scale. Membership of the WCC deepened the ecumenical commitment and enhanced the sense of universality in the life of the Orthodox Churches, and enabled them to make Orthodoxy more broadly visible.

4. While maintaining their Orthodox identity, the Orthodox were also influenced by Western patterns of thought and ways of life. The openness to, and close interaction with, the non-Orthodox world allowed the Orthodox Churches to share, in existential ways, their traditions, theology, and spirituality with Western churches. This, in turn, helped them to relate themselves more meaningfully and reliably to new situations and realities through a process of self-assessment and renewal.

The Orthodox presence in the fellowship of the WCC has always been one of giving and receiving through mutual challenge and enrichment.
This process of living dialogue and growing in fellowship has never been easy and smooth. It has gone through upheavals and tensions. After so many years of ecumenical togetherness, Orthodox Churches still face various problems and concerns. I want to identify some of the basic ones:

1. Since the beginning of their membership in the council, the Orthodox Churches have consistently held that the WCC is a fellowship of churches called essentially for the common search for unity. From this point of view, the WCC is neither above the churches nor does it have authority over the member churches. Rather it provides the churches with a special framework to pray

together, to think together, and to witness together. The WCC is a privileged instrument of the ecumenical movement in which each church retains and bears witness to its identity. With such an understanding of the nature and vocation of the WCC, the Toronto Statement[4] remains the basis for the Orthodox Churches' membership of the council. Therefore, any attempt to review the Toronto Statement may encounter a strong Orthodox objection.

2. The participation of the Orthodox Church in the WCC is based on its ecclesiology. We Orthodox believe that the Orthodox Church is neither a confession, nor one of many confessions. It is the one and undivided church in the unbroken and continuous succession of the sacramental ministry and the Orthodox faith of the apostolic church. Therefore, according to the Orthodox, the problem of church unity must be seen not in terms of interdenominational agreement, nor as church discipline under a centralized authoritarian institution, but as participation in *una sancta*, which was manifested in the early church through the common apostolic tradition. The Orthodox concerns regarding unity are:

◇ First, the Orthodox Churches have great reservations about ecumenical attempts to favour 'intercommunion' and 'interconfessional unions' as the manifestation of visible unity.

◇ Secondly, in spite of continuous endeavours towards unity, the Orthodox Churches feel that this question has not yet been given a central place in the life and programmatic thrusts of the World Council.

◇ Thirdly, the Orthodox fear that the search for unity may never get beyond the study stage. Therefore, a breakthrough of this prevailing impasse should be sought and found.

3. The structural framework, the working style, the language and methodology of the council remain a major hindrance to achieving an efficient Orthodox contribution. Furthermore, the predominant Protestant character of the council, and particularly, questions of representation and decision-making processes often neutralize Orthodox concerns. The Orthodox sometimes find difficulty associating themselves with the priorities of the others. This difficulty, in turn, isolates and alienates the Orthodox.

4. The extending and intensifying 'horizontalism' of the WCC worries the Orthodox Churches. The Orthodox voice strong criti-

cism of the world-oriented and activistic trends that are emerging in various spheres of the council's life and work. Many of the issues and aspects of the seventh assembly in Canberra, including the so-called 'Korean Présentation' of the main theme, manifested, for the Orthodox, the increasing predominance of tendencies and perspectives that the Orthodox consider alien to the nature, identity, and the goals of the WCC. The Orthodox reaction to these aspects and trends, that was expressed in the form of 'Reflections',[5] signalled the growing uneasiness of the Orthodox Churches.

The Orthodox are not against the WCC's social involvement *per se*. However, they are critical of the growing shift in emphasis from theology towards socio-political problems. While some interpret this shift as an expression of a new awareness of the social, economic, and political implications of Christian faith, and the close link between justice and unity of the church, many Orthodox feel it deviates from the basic aim of the council—Christian unity. These are the major problems that the Orthodox are called to wrestle with. These and similar other issues need to be scrutinized carefully and realistically.

The Orthodox Churches are neither outsiders nor newcomers to the council.

His Holiness Athenagoras I, the Ecumenical Patriarch, during his first visit to the headquarters of the WCC in Geneva in 1968, declared: 'We come not as strangers to strangers, but as members of the same family, to this our common home in witness of our Church's profound awareness that it is one of the founding churches of this council and—along with the other sister Orthodox Churches—a deeply engaged and active member of it in the inter-Christian dialogue of love and unity'.[6]

These prophetic words of one of the most prominent Orthodox pioneers of the ecumenical movement are more challenging today than at any time in the history of the Orthodox presence in the WCC. The Orthodox Churches are, in a real sense, among the founding members of the WCC, and as such are not an appendix to the ecumenical fellowship; they are integral to it. With this firm conviction I would like to offer some suggestions for further discussion and action:

1. The ecumenical witness of Orthodoxy can be creative and efficacious only through people. In other words, the Orthodox statements or declarations remain peripheral, having only a super-

ficial and temporary effect, if they are not fully and correctly interpreted and followed up by Orthodox people who are well-versed in ecumenism and are able to enter into critical and meaningful dialogue with non-Orthodox. Therefore, it is decisively important for the future of the Orthodox witness in the ecumenical movement that our churches prepare youth, clergy, and laity—men and women—with ecumenical formation, commitment and vision.

2. We have dealt with almost all the pertinent and major ecumenical issues, and stated our position. But the Orthodox concerns should not remain merely 'Orthodox' concerns. They must be located in the broader context of new ecumenical realities and situations, integrated with others' concerns, and formulated and communicated in an intelligible and relevant way. Such contextualization of Orthodox concerns and perspectives is very much in the tradition of Orthodoxy.

3. World Christendom is becoming increasingly interested in and more knowledgeable about Orthodoxy. Because of this growing openness towards Orthodoxy, churches and their representatives now listen more carefully and sympathetically to Orthodox voices, and take Orthodoxy much more seriously. This significant aspect of present-day ecumenism should not be ignored or taken for granted by the Orthodox Churches.

4. The ecumenical witness of the Orthodox Churches, in my opinion, loses its dynamism and impact if it is reactive rather than positive. The issues that the Orthodox Churches face together with their Christian brothers and sisters should be treated not exclusively in terms of how the Orthodox see them or what the Orthodox Church teaches, but, rather, in terms of how the Orthodox can contribute, in a specific way, towards a common Christian understanding and action. Being critical does not necessarily imply being reactionary. Real contribution is based on a sound and constructive criticism. I believe that such an approach may significantly enhance the Orthodox witness in the WCC and give it impact. It may also generate a keener interest and a genuine trust in ecumenism among the Orthodox at home.

5. In the past the Orthodox were mere observers in the WCC. For many reasons, they did not consider themselves an integral part of the ecumenical fellowship. Often, they felt embarrassed and were unwilling and unable to contribute. Those times have passed now.

The Orthodox Churches are becoming more and more actively present in almost all spheres and at all levels of the council's life and activities. They have started to gain considerable ground in decision-making bodies and processes, and have been given, particularly during the last decade, many opportunities for a broader engagement in the life and work of the WCC. But we need to reorganize our presence and witness in the council. We need to strengthen further the quality of our participation.

After the Canberra assembly, a non-Orthodox delegate wrote to me the following words: 'Many of us left Canberra sharing the reservations expressed in the Orthodox Statement. Of course the answer is for us to get more involved and not to withdraw.' In our ecumenical growth together with other churches we have gone through many difficulties. We have experienced frustrations. We still face problems. But in spite of prevailing ambiguities and tensions, we have reaffirmed that 'we intend to remain faithful to our ecumenical commitment'.[7]

The Orthodox Church rejects an inward-looking parochialism. It firmly believes in ecumenism and considers the WCC as one of the comprehensive and significant manifestations of the ecumenical movement. It is strongly and unequivocally committed to the unity of the church, and considers this the *raison d'être* of the WCC. Therefore, the Orthodox must have a critical attitude in regard to some of the prevailing features and tendencies in the World Council, but they must never incline towards alienation or resignation. For, as we once again made clear in Canberra, the Orthodox Churches are deeply concerned 'about the future of the ecumenical movement, and about the fate of its goals and ideals, as they were formulated by its founders'.[8] Canberra was a reminder that the ecumenical journey is still long and difficult. It was at the same time a real challenge to the Orthodox Churches to move forward from mere contribution to active participation, from critical dialogue to full partnership.[9]

Notes

1. For the encyclicals of Orthodox patriarchs and Orthodox synodical declarations, see Constantin G. Patelos, editor, *The Orthodox Church in the Ecumenical Movement*, WCC, 1978, pages 27–70.

2. Common Orthodox contribution to the ecumenical debate has been made in three different ways: The declarations of Pan-Orthodox conferences, Orthodox statements in connection with major ecumenical meetings, and Orthodox consultations on specific ecumenical themes and issues. For these materials, consult Constantin G. Patelos, editor, *The Orthodox Church in the Ecumenical Movement*, George Tsetsis, editor, *Orthodox Thought: Reports of Orthodox Consultations organized by the WCC, 1975–1982*, WCC, 1983; Orthodox Task Force, editors, *Orthodox Contributions to Nairobi*, WCC, 1975; Gennadios Limouris and Nomikos M. Vaporis, editors, *Orthodox Perspectives on Baptism, Eucharist and Ministry*, Faith and Order Paper 128 and Holy Cross Orthodox Press, 1985; *The New Valamo Consultation: The Ecumenical Nature of the Orthodox Witness*, WCC, 1977; George Lemopoulos, editor, *The Holy Spirit and Mission*, WCC, 1990; Michael Kinnamon, editor, *Signs of the Spirit: Official Report, Seventh Assembly*, WCC and Eerdmans, 1991.

3. For the third time since the breach of ecclesial communion between the Eastern and the Oriental Orthodox Churches, the representatives of these churches engaged in theological dialogue under the umbrella of the Faith and Order of the WCC. Four unofficial consultations were organized between the theologians of the Oriental and Eastern Orthodox Churches. They are: Aarhus, 11–15 August, 1964; Bristol, 25–29 July, 1967; Geneva, 16–21 August, 1970; Addis Ababa, 22–23 January, 1971. Through these meetings, both sides reached a common understanding of their Christological teachings. (For the agreed statements of these meetings, see Paulos Gregorios, William H. Lazareth, Nikos A. Nissiotis, editors, *Does Chalcedon Divide or Unite? Towards Convergence in Orthodox Christology*, WCC, 1981, pages 1–17. The conclusions of these consultations later served as a major reference for the official dialogue between the Oriental and Eastern Orthodox Churches as well as for the unofficial consultations of the Oriental Orthodox and Roman Catholic theologians organized by Pro Oriente.

4. 'The Church, the Churches and the World Council of Churches: the Ecclesiological Significance of the World Council of Churches', in Lukas Vischer, editor, *A Documentary History of the Faith and Order Movement: 1927–1963*, The Bethany Press, 1963, pages 167–76). The Orthodox played a major role in formulating this statement.

5. 'Reflections of Orthodox Participants', in Michael Kinnamon, editor, *Signs of the Spirit: Official Report, Seventh Assembly*, WCC and Eerdmans, 1991, pages 279-82. It is worth mentioning here that the evangelicals as well came up with a similar statement in Canberra: 'Evangelical Perspectives from Canberra' (Ibid., pages 282–86). Remarkably enough, there were a number of converging points in these two statements. This paved the way for informal conversations between evangelicals and Orthodox, which are in process.

6. *The Ecumenical Review*, volume XX, January 1968, number 1, page 86.

7. George Tsetsis, editor, *Orthodox Thought: Reports of Orthodox Consultations organized by the WCC, 1975–1982*, WCC, 1983, page 69.

8. 'Reflections of Orthodox Participants', in Michael Kinnamon, editor, *Signs of the Spirit: Official Report, Seventh Assembly*, WCC and Eerdmans, 1991, page 280.

9.   At the end of its deliberations the consultation produced a final report which deals with the various aspects of the Orthodox involvement in the WCC. This report has not yet been published.

10

Towards a Self-Understanding of the World Council of Churches

This article is the elaboration of some of the observations that I made at a small consultation on 'Towards a Common Understanding of the Nature and Vocation of the WCC', called by the general secretary of the WCC, in Geneva, 29–30 August 1990.[1]

Currently discussions are going on in the World Council of Churches on the 'future' of the WCC. Some describe this debate as reaching 'towards a clearer identity and profile of the WCC'. Others refer to it as 'programmatic reorganization' or simply 'restructuring' of the WCC. The debate in its present stage lacks clarity, focus and orientation.

The emblem of the WCC depicts correctly the nature of the churches' togetherness in the ecumenical movement. It is a pilgrimage by boat. The sea is stormy, the boat is shaky—yet the journey continues. In fact, the ecumenical boat is facing the strongest storms in its forty-two-year history. The world is radically changed and still changing fast. The rapid and spectacular changes have brought new hopes and promises for a better future: they have also immensely increased the fear of human self-destruction and ecological disaster. The emergence of new challenges and crises with all their implications has deeply affected the life and mission of the churches and the ecumenical movement. The WCC is called to witness in an increasingly complex situation in both the churches and the world. It finds itself in a new ecumenical context, one which requires an objective, profound and critical self-analysis—an ecumenical *perestroika*.

The ecumenical movement both challenges and helps the

churches to see and understand themselves in relation to each other and to the world. Therefore, the question is not how the WCC can keep pace with the rhythm of changing times by being up-to-date and relevant in terms of programme, structure or action. The real questions are, first, how can the WCC understand itself as a fellowship of churches committed, through common life and action, to a common search for one church and a common witness to the world? Secondly, what are the implications of the churches' togetherness in the WCC for their life and mission on both a global and a local level?

The WCC: a broken yet growing *koinonia*

The concept of *koinonia*[2] is crucial to the very nature of the churches' fellowship in the WCC. It is important to bear in mind the important distinction that exists between the ecumenical movement, the World Council of Churches and the Ecumenical Centre in Geneva. The WCC is not the Ecumenical Centre. It is only the administrative centre of the movement. The WCC is not the ecumenical movement; it is one (albeit the most comprehensive) manifestation of it. Furthermore, the WCC is not the source of ecumenism. It is only one of its organic expressions. The ecumenical movement cannot be confined to any organization. It transcends all forms and structures. The WCC is, to use a generally accepted expression, a 'privileged instrument' of the ecumenical movement.

Two years after its foundation, the WCC attempted to define itself. The well-known Toronto statement pointed out in clear terms the major aspects and special character of this fellowship. It spelled out what the WCC is and is not. According to Toronto, the WCC is by its very nature and mandate a fellowship of divided churches committed to the fuller and visible manifestation of unity. Therefore, the WCC does not intend to become a 'super-church' or 'world church'. It does not negotiate unions between the churches; it brings the churches closer to each other in 'solidarity', 'brotherly relationships', 'conversation', 'co-operation' and 'common witness'. Membership of the council does not imply 'mutual recognition', however, it leads the churches to identify 'elements of the true church' in each other. Furthermore, the WCC is not to 'usurp' the function of the churches or 'to control' them or 'to legislate' for them, thus becoming 'a centralized administrative authority'.

Toronto is crucial for the self-understanding of the WCC. The question is: does the identity of the WCC as described by Toronto still remain valid? After forty-two years of shared life and common witness, how does the WCC understand itself today? I would like to make the following observations:

1. The WCC has developed as an organization rather than as a fellowship. Its public image is one of organization, a sort of UN of the churches where the churches voice their concerns, pursue their interests, protect their rights, expose their needs and appeal for solidarity. Such a misconception of the WCC needs to be strongly challenged. Organization is unavoidable and, in fact, indispensable for a universal fellowship of such size and composition. But the WCC is not an inter-church organization nor an association of churches. It is a fellowship with a specific nature and a definite goal. The Holy Spirit is the generator, sustainer and leader of it. This unique character of the WCC has to be constantly and clearly spelled out.

2. The WCC is not merely a platform for common action; it is a fellowship of prayer. Hence, spirituality is integral to the nature of the council. It seems to me that the council has almost lost its sense of the centrality of prayer. Within its hectic life and heavy schedule, worship has moved to the periphery. The spiritual dimension of the council's work has been overshadowed by practical concerns. It is vital that spirituality as a quality of life and witness be recovered, in different ways and forms, in all areas and at different levels of the council's life, thought and work. Otherwise, the council loses its specific identity and basic vocation and becomes merely an administrative structure.

3. The WCC is not a federation of churches where the churches simply co-exist. It is a fellowship which leads the churches to critical self-assessment, mutual understanding and correction. It establishes interaction and interrelation between the churches. Therefore, it is a fellowship that presupposes mutuality: mutual sharing, commitment, challenge and accountability. It is a broken, yet growing, *koinonia*; it grows through a process of giving and receiving. This is one of the significant features of the WCC. The council, particularly during the last two decades, has stimulated and enhanced this common, enriching process of growth among the member churches, also at local levels, through mutual openness and sharing. Mutuality has become, beyond its programmatic and structural

expressions, a way of thinking, living and acting that has penetrated almost all domains of the churches' lives. In fact, in many parts of the world and particularly at local level, ecumenism has become now almost equivalent to mutual sharing of resources, concerns, suffering and joy.

4. The WCC is not a mere framework for collaboration between the churches on matters of common interest. It is a constant reminder of the brokenness of the body of Christ and a challenge to grow in full unity. The WCC is a fellowship of churches based not on a common ecclesiology, but a common commitment to work together for visible unity. Because of the very nature of the council and the goal it strives for, tensions, divergences and even polarizations achieve a measure of reconciliation in this fellowship. In fact, the WCC has always acted as one family, though a divided one.

5. The WCC has provided the churches with the opportunity to revive and re-affirm their ethnic, cultural and confessional identities. At the same time it has brought the churches out of their parochialism and given them the sense and the experience of the universal dimension of the Church of God. In fact, the local and the universal have entered into dialogical relationship in the life, thought and work of the council. They have strengthened, enriched, and challenged each other.

Besides the significant achievements of the WCC mentioned above, we must also acknowledge its limitations, deficiencies and shortcomings. The WCC is not yet the kind of fellowship we are looking for. It is a provisional fellowship. Therefore, the churches should not feel wholly comfortable in it. They are far from the goal they are struggling for. To what extent are the churches faithful in their praxis to the commitment they have made by their very presence in the WCC?

Let me, at this juncture, touch on some major issues that, sooner or later, the council will have to wrestle with.

The WCC is not a reality above, apart from, or parallel to the churches. It is the churches-in-fellowship.[3] It has become a home for the churches where they feel themselves closer to each other as members of the same family. It has provided an appropriate framework for the churches' common reflection and action. But how far do the member churches actually identify themselves with the WCC? This is indeed a major concern, that needs to be addressed seriously. The widening gap between the WCC and the member churches, in my judgment, is not due to what is sometimes superficially referred to as 'lack of communication'.

The following factors have been decisive in creating such an unhealthy situation: the WCC's emphasis on global issues with little concern for their local implications; the centralized structures of the WCC, which do not touch the actual life of the churches; the churches' increasingly direct involvement in national issues as well as their active role in local and regional ecumenism.

A concerted effort has to be made by both the WCC and the member churches to bridge the gap. Ecumenical education ought to be an integral part of our theological education, pastoral work, and missionary activities. The awareness of belonging to a fellowship of churches must be strengthened. Our people should know that the WCC is not the ecumenical centre, the staff, the sub-units, the programmes, the committees, or those who are part of the decision-making processes in Geneva. The WCC is essentially those who are at home, the grassroots people, the local congregation. No doubt unity remains the *raison d'être* of the council. But the enthusiasm of the early days has now faded and the search for unity has lost momentum. The emergence of new priorities has diluted the concern for unity to such a degree that sometimes people in the WCC—in particular the Orthodox—have to go on focusing on the centrality of the question of unity. In our common search for unity we are presently exposed to four possible dangers.

◇ First, unity is not only a goal before us, it is also a reality behind us. Therefore, an exclusively eschatological approach is not correct. Unity is a gift as well as a call of God. We have lost its fullness. We have it now in its brokenness. We are called to live and manifest what we have as well as work for its fullness.

◇ Secondly, there are actually two tendencies in the WCC, namely to look at unity mainly in its horizontal-existential dimension, and to conceive it as a vertical reality unrelated to other issues that the churches confront in their life and mission. These two approaches need to be taken in their intimate interconnectedness. Otherwise they may greatly endanger the nature of our fellowship.

◇ Thirdly, we should not confuse the communion of confessional bodies with the communion the churches share in the WCC. We must not make an easy analogy. We are still in pre-eucharistic and pre-conciliar communion.

◇ Fourthly, not only do the churches now give priority to bilateral dialogues as the most efficient and reliable way of seeking unity, but they also tend to question the council's efforts towards unity, arguing that they lead nowhere.

The WCC has to take these factors seriously. We have, in fact, come out, through the work of Faith and Order, with a number of challenging models of unity. But can we agree on a model of unity when we still have different understandings of the nature of unity? Can we possibly reach a common understanding of the nature of unity when we still have different ecclesiological teachings on the nature of the church? We need to develop ecumenical perspectives in ecclesiology.[4] I consider this crucial for the future of the council.

The WCC is not a 'super-church'. It neither replaces nor represents the churches. But does the churches' fellowship within the framework of the WCC imply some degree of 'ecclesial reality'? The churches have different understandings concerning the nature and the degree of the WCC's ecclesiality. Some see it in the function of the WCC, namely as a functional rather than a static reality. Others identify it with the goal of the council. There are also those who deny any ecclesial dimension to the WCC. This question was raised again, directly or indirectly, during the last two central committee meetings. It seems to me that it will soon become one of the major issues for the WCC and it will have to take a critical look at itself, its nature, its basis and mandate, its self-understanding vis-à-vis the new ecumenical situations and the exigencies of the present world. In other words, the question of looking afresh at the Toronto statement will become a priority on the ecumenical agenda.

Currently there are two emerging views in the WCC. For some churches Toronto is outdated, therefore, it must be revised. For others, including the Orthodox, Toronto is the best description so far of the nature and the vocation of the WCC. Undoubtedly, Toronto was a significant achievement as the first serious attempt to clarify the special character of the churches' togetherness in the WCC. It remains a major point of reference.

But Toronto is not sacrosanct. It was never intended to be. It needs constant rereading and reimplementation. In fact, in many respects we are far beyond Toronto. In some respects we are before Toronto. The question is not a revision of Toronto as such. It is not as simple as that. The question is: after a long and often painful process of developing reciprocal understanding and trust, have we not reached a decisive stage in our growth in ecumenical maturity where we must somehow restate, re-affirm, and re-evaluate the nature and the goal of the WCC *vis-à-vis* our common commitment to the one church and in the context of the present realities and challenges of the world? I know this is a still untouched and, for some churches, an untouchable issue. But somehow we have to face it with courage and humility. Facing the issue does not mean solving it. But it would itself be a promising step forward.[5]

Recently we have heard some voices in the churches and in the council as well that the WCC does not know where it is going, that it has no vision. I do not share this pessimism. The WCC has a vision.[6] Unity, mission, *diakonia*, justice and renewal must continue to constitute the major and basic ingredients of the multi-faceted and multi-dimensional vision of the WCC. The WCC is the common response of the churches to the call of God to grow in unity. Therefore, the WCC is a *koinonia* of divided churches which constantly calls the churches to the goal of 'visible unity in one faith' and in 'one eucharistic fellowship'. It is a *koinonia* that generates hope and reconcilition, and struggles for liberation, justice and peace and for true humanity.

The WCC: a *koinonia* of shared relationship

Relationship is the sustaining power of the WCC. It is an inseparable dimension of its nature. The WCC is not a source of ecumenism, a place that generates ecumenism; it is rather a fellowship that also receives ecumenism. It has to discern the signs of the Holy Spirit in the churches and in the world and manifest them through its life and witness. The WCC becomes a mere organization if it fails to perceive itself as a continually up-building and growing *koinonia* through shared relationship.

Relationship implies communication and interpretation. In fact, the WCC has made significant advances in this area. It has broadened the scope of its relationship, sophisticated its communication network, and strengthened its mechanism of interpretation. But in spite of these important steps, the WCC's relationships remain, to a large degree, disorganized and inefficient. They need basic revision and restructuring. Let me identify some of the major aspects and areas of the WCC's relationships and offer a few remarks:

RELATIONSHIP WITH THE MEMBER CHURCHES

This is the most vital area of the WCC's relationships. The WCC has to derive its life and witness from the churches and has to relate itself back to the churches. Therefore, beyond the routine communication with church leadership, the WCC must develop the kind of living relationship by which it can listen to the churches more directly and integrate the ecumenical vision more efficiently at all levels of the churches' life. The ecclesial reality cannot be reduced to the institutional church. Reaching the *laos*, the people of God, has to be the driving force and should constitute the criterion and the goal of the WCC's relationship with the member churches.

The member churches must take the WCC more seriously, engaging more fully and responsibly in the life and work of the council. This engagement is of ecisive importance for the future of the council. For many churches the WCC is a reality outside their actual life. The goals, concerns and hopes of the council are not existentially experienced by the churches. The ecumenical fellowship the churches share in the WCC is not taken back home and articulated concretely at the local level. The churches expect a great deal from the WCC, but they give very little back. This is a dilemma within the ecumenical fellowship which is mainly due, in my view, to the lack of concrete requirements from the member churches for their membership in the council, on the one hand, and, as I said earlier, to the growing importance given by the member churches to regional and local ecumenism on the other.

The WCC will continue to face with increasing acuteness the questions of participation and representation. In fact, whatever steps the council takes in this respect the imbalances will exist in one form or another. They are part of the ecumenical fellowship. Thus, the Orthodox churches will always criticize the lack of necessary conditions in the WCC which would enable them to act on equal footing with other member churches. The Third World, women, and youth will never find their concerns and aspirations fully satisfied. The decision-makers will continue to come predominantly from bigger and wealthier churches in the North. The WCC, in its turn, will continue to give special consideration to confessional, geographical, gender and age factors. Furthermore, the staff will always try to play, for various reasons, an important role in leadership selection and decision-making processes. These concerns and practices will have their negative repercussions on the quality of the council at both leadership and staff levels.

How can the churches make their representation a real participation? This is a major issue that the churches must tackle. The churches' relationship to the WCC is one of commitment. The WCC's relationship to the churches is one of service. This relationship of commitment and service is sustained by mutual accountability, questioning, and responsibility. Serving the churches is not only doing what the churches want, but also doing what the churches themselves cannot do. In crisis situations a leadership and prophetic role is required of the WCC.

RELATIONSHIP WITH THE ROMAN CATHOLIC CHURCH

This should remain an important dimension of the council's life. Through the Joint Working Group the WCC's relationship and collaboration with the Roman Catholic Church has significantly expanded and deepened. But the lack of major breakthrough may bring this relationship to stagnation. The bilateral relations and dialogues between some of the member churches and world communions and the Roman Catholic Church are much more promising than the one between the WCC and the Roman Catholic Church. Furthermore, the Roman Catholic Church and even some of the member churches are taking these dialogues much more seriously than the WCC, because the latter cannot speak for the churches and, as such, it cannot go beyond the accepted limits in its relationship with the Roman Catholic Church. How can we deal with this?

Besides this problem, we face three major concerns in the relationship between the WCC and the Roman Catholic Church: first, the Roman Catholic insistence on Rome-centred ecumenism in spite of its affirmation of one ecumenical movement; secondly, the selective and limited nature of its collaboration with the council; thirdly, its great reservation over membership of the WCC. As long as these problems remain the WCC will face ambiguity and difficulty in its ecumenical co-operation with the Roman Catholic Church.

But we have to continue this relationship with renewed commitment, identifying new areas of collaboration, embarking on joint programmes, and organizing joint ecumenical events. The relationship between Geneva and Rome is not a relationship between two centres of ecumenism. Ecumenism has no institutional centre. Jesus Christ is the centre of ecumenism. The WCC and the Roman Catholic Church are called to be full partners in the one ecumenical movement. Their close collaboration will determine the future of the ecumenical movement.

RELATIONSHIP WITH CHRISTIAN GROUPS AND MOVEMENTS

The ecumenical movement has now come out of the boundaries of the institutional churches and become a reality with which many people identify themselves. Hence the WCC must address itself to a broader ecumenical spectrum, somehow also dealing with non-institutional Christian movements and groups. I know that many churches would not like to see these movements or groups—which are either rejected or marginalized by the churches—taken seriously by the WCC. fBut the WCC cannot avoid them for at least three reasons:

◇ First, they have grown and expanded in many parts of the world and have gained considerable ground and sympathy in many churches and particularly among youth and laity.

◇ Secondly, they are challenging and questioning those patterns of thought, ways of life, and structures of decision-making which, in their view, make the church irrelevant to the new realities and situations of the world.

◇ Thirdly, they are actively involved in struggles for justice, peace and human rights, as well as in renewal movements.

The WCC is a council of churches. It cannot become a council of movements or groups. The churchly character of the WCC must be maintained. In other words, the WCC cannot become a forum for these groups and movements. Therefore, the question is not to give them some kind of recognition or status within the constituency of the WCC, but rather to enter into critical and informal dialogue with them as well as to challenge the churches to do the same. The WCC has to be aware that dealing with these movements and groups independently from the churches may create tensions within the churches and may even lead to the disintegration of the council. Therefore, the WCC has to be always selective and critically receptive as well as sensitive towards the concerns of the churches.

RELATIONSHIP WITH NATIONAL AND REGIONAL COUNCILS AND WORLD COMMUNIONS

National and regional councils are important manifestations of the ecumenical movement. They are, in a sense, local and regional 'extensions' of the WCC. Relationships with these ecumenical bodies are of pivotal importance for four main reasons.

◇ First, the ecumenical reality in its local setting is authentically and visibly articulated through these bodies.

◇ Secondly, the churches are more existentially and firmly attached to these ecumenical structures than to the WCC.

◇ Thirdly, due to the increasing participation of the Roman Catholic Church, the councils may become proper contexts for a deeper WCC-Roman Catholic collaboration at local and regional levels.

◇ Fourthly, these councils may also establish dynamic interaction between global and local ecumenism, which is, in fact, a missing dimension in the WCC.

The WCC ought to pursue the following major objectives in its relationship with these ecumenical bodies: avoiding duplication and contradiction; articulating mutual concerns at local, regional and global levels; giving more credibility and visibility to the churches' ecumenical fellowship on various levels and in different areas of ecclesial life; enhancing the churches' search for visible unity; delegating some responsibilities—those which have a regional character and scope—to regional and national councils. I believe that such a close working relationship will allow the WCC to secure the tangible support of these councils as well as to focus its energy on major global issues. It will also strengthen the role of regional and national councils in this new period of the history of the ecumenical movement marked by a growing shift from global to local ecumenism.

In its relationship with the world communions, the WCC must give particular attention to bilateral dialogues that have acquired so much importance during the last decade. The WCC's role may be twofold:

◇ First, in view of the proliferation and diversification of dialogues—often with no connection with each other—the WCC can become an appropriate forum for creative interaction.

◇ Secondly, this may lead the WCC to identify some of the major issues of the ongoing dialogues and tackle them in broader ecumenical perspectives. Faith and Order can play a leading part in achieving this.

The WCC is, in one way or another, in constant touch with the realities and problems of the world. It is called to identify itself with those realities or actions which are compatible with the gospel message as well as to denounce publicly those situations or actions which are against the principles of Christian faith and the teaching of Christ's church. Neutrality or silence is disobedience to Christ. Herein lies, I think, the unique identity of the WCC. In fact, the WCC has been articulate at this point. It has also been, to some extent, ambiguous in its choice of issues and in its position-taking.

The WCC, in faithfulness to its vocation, should transcend all kinds of marginal and temporal considerations and say things clearly as the occasion requires. Such courageous commitment may, in some cases, not help to solve the crisis; it may even worsen the situation. But I believe that it will help immensely on a long-term basis and will give credibility to the WCC's public image. Human considerations may create tensions or may even divide the churches. But faithfulness to the gospel unites them and impels the WCC to uphold justice and peace and the cause of the victimized and marginalized.

The WCC: a *koinonia* of reflection-action

The WCC is also a growing *koinonia* of reflection and action. These are not two successive and independent stages, but interrelated and interdependent aspects of the same process. They are the ingoing and the outgoing of ecumenical fellowship. The programmes of the WCC are the locus where this reflection-action takes place. Theological reflection-action should undergird all the council's programmes since such programmes are the instruments and the concrete manifestations of the WCC's self-understanding and sharing of relationships. Hence, any self-understanding of the WCC and any reorganizing of its relationships will have a direct bearing on its programmatic thrusts and priorities.

In fact, the programmes of the WCC were, for various reasons, considerably broadened and diversified, particularly after the Uppsala assembly. Although some serious efforts were made after the Nairobi assembly towards a reassessment of the programmes, the need for programmatic reorganization remains absolutely necessary. This has to be done on the basis of well-established criteria and according to clearly-defined guidelines. In my judgment, the following factors and concerns have to be taken into consideration:

1. The programmes of the WCC must primarily and necessarily reflect the needs of the member churches. In other words, the concerns of the churches should echo through the programmes. Such concerns are the *raison d'être* of any programme in the council. They have to be conceived and developed to enable the churches to grow towards fuller unity, and they should be responsive to the needs and priorities of the churches. Therefore, no programmatic priority should be imposed on the churches. The priority must emerge from the actual situation of the churches.

2. Not only should the programmes of the WCC become the programmes of the churches, the churches ought to be part of them, becoming involved at all stages and in all aspects of the programmes. This implies the development of participatory programmes and not office-centred and merely study-oriented programmes. I believe that the churches can bring more substantial participation in the life and work of the WCC through programmes rather than through the constituted bodies of the council. Also, participatory types of programmes may help both the churches and the WCC immensely in establishing more direct and living contacts with local realities.

3. The WCC should listen to the churches with one ear and to the world with the other. The agenda of the churches is not necessarily the world's and vice versa. The programmes of the WCC cannot be exclusively churchy or worldly. I am aware of the strong criticism voiced by some of the churches that the WCC has become too 'worldly'. But we cannot neglect either. Nor can we draw a clear line of demarcation between the two. It is vitally important that in the WCC's programmatic thrusts a dynamic interaction be established between the churches' priorities, and the urgent needs and acute problems of the world which call for Christian action.

4. The programmes must have a clear focus. Ambiguity, vagueness, lack of clarity, and duplication must be avoided. The WCC has become a powerful body which tries to cope with a wide range of problems. This broadening of the scope of the WCC programmatic engagement gives a sense of triumphalism to the council; it also endangers its identity and obscures its vision. The multi-dimen-

sional activities of the WCC must be preserved. But the WCC cannot deal with all the problems of the world. It should accept its limits and limitations. It has to be selective. It must clearly identify its main emphasis. This implies constant regrouping, revision, and simplification of the programmes in their structural, financial and staffing aspects and implications.

5. Special efforts should be made not to overwhelm the programmes with studies and paperwork. The programmes become mere study projects if they are not ultimately, in one way or another, oriented towards action, convergence, consensus or reception. Reflection and action must be maintained as an integrated whole. Any reflection process, if it is not sooner or later translated into some kind of concrete action or convergence calling for 'reception'—the churches' response and participation, loses its *raison d'être* within the programmatic priorities of the WCC.

6. We are living in an interdependent world. The issues that the WCC is wrestling with are not, strictly speaking, independent issues. They are intimately interconnected, but the interrelatedness of the issues has not been spelled out at the programmatic level. The programmes simply co-exist in the council. There is a tendency to departmentalize the programmatic concerns rather than to see them as integral parts of a whole. Therefore, beyond the interaction between the programmes, and collaboration between the sub-units, a particular consideration ought to be given to interdisciplinary programmes. The development of such programmes may also help towards the tightening of programmatic thrusts, spelling out the focuses of programmes and minimizing the financial burden of the council.

7. The programmes' feasibility, viability and relevance must be constantly checked. Some of the ongoing programmes have lost much of their impact and have been reduced to routine activities. They need to be reviewed, and, if necessary, simply dropped. The Central Committee must have a programme review committee to discuss the programme priorities and to screen programme prosposals on a regular basis.

8. The increasing emphasis on global issues has moved local concerns and priorities to the periphery of the programmes. The WCC should provide enough room in its programmatic thrusts both for the local and global priorities as well as for their interaction.

The local and contextual issues need to be treated in a global perspective without jeopardizing their local dimension, and the local implications of global issues must be clearly singled out. The local should be neither at the expense of the global nor dominated by the global. Exclusive globalism and parochialism must be avoided.

9. The programmes of the WCC are time-bound, issue-oriented, and financially-conditioned. We cannot avoid these limitations. The WCC must, however, devise types of programmes that provide an eschatological dimension and vision to the WCC's work and orient the council towards the future. In other terms, the WCC's reflection-action process must have some kind of continuity. It must project the nature and the basis of the WCC and be sustained by the vision of one church giving new hope for the future, new shape to our common goal and renewed impetus to our common struggle for justice and peace.

10.The WCC has no theology of its own. The development of an 'ecumenical' theology is neither possible nor the aim of the council. The WCC will continue to accommodate, in its theological thinking, various theologies, cultures and traditions. In fact, this is one of the most remarkable aspects of the WCC's life and witness. But we need quality, integrity and coherence in the diversified theological thinking and methodology of the council. Therefore, the development of creative interaction between various confessional and contextual theologies in the council, on the one hand, and the theological realities and concerns of the member churches, on the other, is vitally important.

11.In spite of the expansion of the WCC's membership and the growing role of the Orthodox and of Third-World churches, the WCC continues to be predominantly Western, more specifically European, in its structure, style and spirituality, and Protestant in its theology. Only a small élite in the member churches have access to the language, thinking, and life-style of the WCC. The council must slowly get rid of Eurocentrism. Such a move will, undoubtedly, give more relevance and reliability to the council's programmes as well as increase the degree of its acceptability by the member churches.

12.The WCC is not represented to the churches and the public in terms of its overall image, but in a fragmented and departmentalized way. For some it is Faith and Order, for others CWME or CCIA, for many CICARWS, an agency that sponsors projects. In my view, this misconception is largely due to the existence of multiple decision centres in the council, the lack of necessary integration between the programmes, sub-units and overarching concerns of the council, and the absence of effective ways and means of interpreting the WCC as one fellowship with a common vision. It is crucial that this work of the council be conceived, expressed and implemented as a comprehensive whole in its spiritual, prophetic and diaconic dimensions and manifestations.

All these observations point to our need for a more comprehensive and clearer definition of the nature and role of programmes in the WCC. In fact, we need programmes that deal with people and touch the actual life of the churches, that are simple, transparent, dynamic, and flexible enough to be able to respond to new challenges and realities. We need programmes that help the churches to carry on with a new awareness of their God-given mission in the world of today; that strengthen the churches' fellowship and advance it further on the way towards visible unity.[7]

Vis-à-vis the new realities and exigencies of the world and the growing concerns of the churches, it is vitally important that the WCC embark on a process of comprehensive and critical reassessment of the churches' ecumenical togetherness in the WCC, leading to a deeper commitment to the vision of the ecumenical movement. This process of critical self-understanding should not become a Geneva-based process, but the churches' process.

◇ First, the member churches have to enter this common attempt of self-understanding as one fellowship committed to one and the same vision with a sense of common responsibility and partnership.

◇ Secondly, it must not be reduced to a programmatic restructuring, but must embrace the whole of the WCC in its constitutional, functional, programmatic, relational, thematic, and structural aspects.

◇ Thirdly, it must not be conceived as a study process, but as an action-oriented process. Its decisions and findings must be implemented step by step according to a well-established procedure and timetable.The Canberra assembly must be a decisive stage in this process.[8]

Notes

1. It appeared in *The Ecumenical Review*, special issue on 'The Ecumenical Future and the WCC—A Dialogue of Dreams and Visions', volume 42, number 1, January 1991, pages 11–21.

2. The concept of *koinonia* acquired a special focus in the assembly of Canberra, and particularly in its statement on unity (Michael Kinnamon, editor, *Signs of the Spirit: Official Report, Seventh Assembly*, WCC and Eerdmans, 1991, pages 172–74) I believe that *koinonia* will become a major topic on the ecumenical agenda in the post-Canberra period. It is significant to note that the forthcoming Faith and Order World Conference in 1993 will have as its theme: 'Towards Communion in Faith, Life and Witness'.

3. I have also reflected on the nature of the WCC as a fellowship of divided churches in my first Moderator's Report to the Central Committee of the WCC, 16–25 August, 1991, Geneva, Switzerland. The report will appear in *The Ecumenical Review*.

4. I want to note here with special satisfaction that the Canberra assembly affirmed the crucial importance of ecclesiology for the unity of the church and for the future of the ecumenical movement. With this expectation it recommended the Faith and Order to make 'The Ecumenical Perspective of Ecclesiology' one of its priorities for the next period (Michael Kinnamon, editor, *Signs of the Spirit: Official Report, Seventh Assembly*, WCC and Eerdmans, 1991, page 99).

5. In recent years the Orthodox have expressed, individually and collectively, strong reservations about any attempt to revise Toronto. They did the same in their last statement of the Chambesy consultation (pages 131, 146).

6. In this context it is worth reading my report to the last Central Committee of the WCC which was entirely devoted to the description of the ecumenical vision as it has been re-emerged from Canberra, and the re-affirmation of the vital dimensions of the ecumenical vision.

7. In response to the recommendation of the Canberra assembly the Central Committee in its last meeting (16–25 August, 1991) adopted a new programmatic structure and established new priorities for the WCC. Some of the concerns that I have touched in this article have been taken care of in this new programmatic framework. Any programmatic structure is not a project on the paper. It is neither a fixed, frozen system. It must be tested in the actual life. It is important, therefore, that in the process of implementation, the constantly changing realities and priorities of the churches and the societies be seriously taken into consideration.

8. Canberra paid a special attention to this issue. The process will continue after the assembly. In fact, the last meeting of the Central Committee raised the issue. It will become a major item on the agenda of the meeting of the Central Committee in August 1992.

STUDIES IN EVANGELISM, MISSION AND DEVELOPMENT
Published by Regnum Books in association with
Lynx Communications

Sharing Jesus in the Two-Thirds World
Vinay Samuel and Chris Sugden (editors)

The collected papers from the conference that set the direction for
contemporary evangelical mission theology. They look at christology
and mission in numerous contexts: Islam, Buddhism, African
Traditional Religions, Latin America, Western scholarly debate . . .

268 pages, paperback, ISBN 0 7459 2683 5
UK price £5.95

Theology and Identity
Kwame Bediako

How can African Christians today live and worship in a way which is
both true to the gospel and authentically African? In this major study,
leading Ghanaian theologian Kwame Bediako looks to Christians of
the first centuries AD for the answers.

512 pages, paperback, ISBN 0 7459 2684 3
UK price £19.95

Beyond Canberra
Bruce Nicholls and Bong Rin Ro (editors)

Leading theologians reflect on the themes studied at the WCC
conference in Canberra and look at how different branches of the
church can learn from each others' strengths.

Publishing January 1993, ISBN 0 7459 2686 X
UK price £12.50

Biblical Images for Leaders and Followers
David W. Bennett

Leadership is a key issue in all mission and ministry. Many today base their approach to leadership on management studies. But what has the New Testament to teach us? This detailed series of word studies gives the answers.

In preparation, ISBN 0 7459 2688 6

The Story of Faith Missions
Klaus Fiedler

The faith missions have had a major role for more than a century in spreading the church worldwide. This substantial study tells the story in detail and examines the standing of faith missions today.

In preparation, ISBN 0 7459 2687 8

Order these titles from your bookshop or from:

Lynx Communications,
Peter's Way
Sandy Lane West,
Oxford, OX4 5HG,
England

or fax with your credit card number:
UK: 0865 747568
International: +44 865 747568

Add for postage and packing:
£3   (UK)
£5   (Europe)
£7   (Rest of the world)